by

William H. Considine

with Ron Kirksey

Table of Contents

A Note from Jim Tressel

Bill and Becky Considine have spent a lifetime in their hometown of Akron, Ohio, as profound difference makers.

Society seems to suggest that leadership is a position one holds. However, the Considines believe that leadership is the action taken to serve others. For decades, under Bill's leadership at Akron Children's Hospital, thousands of children and their families have been served at crucial moments in their lives.

The "Considine service" does not stop there. Countless communities have enjoyed the leadership, service, and benefits of

From left, Jim and Ellen Tressel, Becky and Bill Considine.

the "Considine contribution." Northeast Ohio, the great state of Ohio, and our nation are better because of the Considine family.

Enjoy and learn from the leadership and service lessons in this special book. Your opportunity to serve others will be enhanced.

Jim Tressel

President, Youngstown State University

Foreword

William Considine is old school.

He has been in healthcare for over 45 years, most of that career spent in one job, as CEO of Akron Children's Hospital. He works in the town where he grew up. He lives in the state where he earned his master's in health administration (The Ohio State University). He is immensely popular in his community and has been accorded honor after honor in his career. As one of the longest-serving hospital CEOs in the United States, Bill has led Akron Children's exponential growth to become the largest pediatric healthcare provider in northern Ohio, with more than one million annual patient visits in over 60 locations. He has also expanded the scope of services to include advanced cardiac care, neurology and neurosurgery, neonatology, orthopedics, intensive care, behavioral health, maternal fetal medicine, genetics, infectious disease, and the state's first pediatric sports medicine center. Bill is actively involved in numerous healthcare, education, and cultural organizations at local, state, and national levels. He is a Fellow in the American College of Healthcare Executives and a past board chairman of the National Association of Children's Hospitals and Related Institutions, the Children's Miracle Network, the Child Health Corporation of America, and more.

All of that speaks to a distinguished career, but for me, what sets him apart—and what this book reveals—is his character. I've known him for many years. He is a man of honor, intense feeling, dedication to patients and staff, vision, and, not least, great humor. He writes of his job as if it were new and exciting—38 years after his start date. The many CEOs I hear complaining about burnout after a few years of running an organization should pay attention to what he has to say.

I have written extensively on leadership, including a couple of my own books. As Bill says, "You know a leader when you see one," and Bill is a leader. He listens, he truly cares about people, he inspires. Using his own words, true leaders like him can "make the impossible seem possible." Though, of course, being humble, he would never speak of himself that way.

This book is for anyone who is a leader or wants to be a leader, whether in healthcare or some other field. It is filled with common sense, practical insight on how to set the course of an organization and how to inspire those who report to you and those who serve you.

Bill writes about what children have taught him regarding purpose. Of course, one child stands out—Angie. She was admitted to the hospital with leukemia when she was nine years old. She didn't survive her illness, but in four short years at Akron Children's, she left a legacy for her elders. As someone who has recently battled leukemia, I was struck by Bill's description of Angie's positive attitude, summed up as "I have no time for bad hair days."

"People don't realize how much we learn and how much gratification we get from the Angies who come into our lives," Bill writes. "They show us the real world, where business strategy meets life. We are better people—and leaders—when these life decisions take their seat at the strategy sessions."

There is much to recommend in this book, most of it coming back to values. The chapter on humor is important, and the willingness to share humor with others is key. Humility and humor, of course, go hand in hand—and any leader who lacks either does not fulfill the description of a true leader. The chapter on storytelling highlights another core element of leadership: You must be able to communicate the mission and vision of your organization to all stakeholders if it is to succeed.

Bill also writes on another topic near and dear to my heart, which is being a role model for employees. From everything I have heard, he has been that and much more.

I love his description of the signs that reflect the organization's heart, words like *trust, purpose, beliefs, respect.* He quotes Goethe: "Treat people as if they were what they ought to be and you help them become what they are capable of being."

Finally, I like Bill's attitude as to how leaders should set the right tone of leadership. You must be prepared, honest, humble, and caring.

Service above self is a mantra Bill lives by, and it's evident in the culture he has helped create for employees. He spends time roaming the halls, meeting patients, families, and employees as much as he can.

He is nearer the end of his career than the beginning or even midpoint, but he is still inspired by his job. He often looks at a framed suncatcher resting on his windowsill, given to him by Angie's mom after Angie died.

"It reminds me every day that our work as a children's hospital is never done," he says.

As I mentioned, the man is old school. I highly recommend you read this book.

Charles S. Lauer
Former publisher, *Modern Healthcare* magazine
Winnetka, Illinois
December 2016

My dear friend Chuck Lauer, former publisher of *Modern Healthcare* magazine, passed away as this book was being prepared for publishing. He was a man for all seasons and a gift to all of us. His words and actions have created a lasting legacy and example that will benefit everyone on their life journeys. His foreword to this book on leadership now takes on special meaning. Chuck embodied the elements of leadership, and I am forever grateful he came into my life. As you read these chapters, reflect on the life of Chuck Lauer, and your life will be enriched.

William Considine
May 2017

Chuck S. Lauer (1930 – 2017)

Introduction

"No bad hair days"

Angie came to us with leukemia when she was nine years old. That's not unusual. At Akron Children's Hospital, helping sick children is what we do. People I meet are often amazed that we can be around such anxiety, pain, and grief yet still keep our humanity.

Specifically, they ask me how, after 45 years in healthcare and 38 years as president and CEO of Akron Children's, I am able to stay fresh and engaged as a leader in what seems like an occupation prone to burnout.

It's true that in our work we have periodic unhappy endings. But we also witness miracles. All of us—staff, physicians, nurses, technicians, researchers, and administrators—are professional healers. What we do is a mission rather than a job.

People don't realize how much we learn and how much gratification we get from the Angies who come into our lives. They show us the real world, where business strategy meets life. We are better people—and leaders—when these life decisions take their seat at strategy sessions.

Patients like Angie and the people who care for them teach me leadership lessons every day. Angie, for instance, kept her positive outlook through rounds of chemotherapy, radiation treatments, and long stays at the hospital—through a total disruption of her life and her family's world. Yet this profoundly ill child reversed the roles of patient and caregiver. She helped us—the healers—heal and cope. Angie took advantage of the hospital's art therapy program to make suncatchers, which she gave to staff and visitors.

Angie Swords

Her mantra was, "I have no time for bad hair days." She understood that time was running out. We adopted the phrase to help us focus on our work, to understand that we can take nothing for granted and to use every moment to serve our miracle children.

Angie and her suncatchers brought light into countless rooms and lives. My job stays fresh because these children keep me grounded, yet constantly amazed. This book is designed to pass on those lessons in a way that any leader can adapt them in any organization.

Obviously, not everyone leads an enterprise with the ongoing drama inherent in a children's hospital. But I've discovered that an invisible force unites all good organizations. A large part of your job as a leader is to identify that force, or spirit, to nourish it and communicate it to every member of your organization. The information in this book can help you become the leader of just such a spirit-infused organization.

Perhaps it seems a reach to translate the leadership lessons from healing children into a practical strategy for private businesses, nonprofit organizations, universities, or other institutions. But we all tend to overcomplicate the practice of leadership and management.

In a children's hospital, you see life stripped down to the basics. You can't fool children. We see more clearly when we look through their eyes. They tell us whether we are on track with our leadership strategy because the results directly affect them in the most basic ways. They show us not only how to lead but also how to become a complete person—how to promote a values-based work environment and operational strategy.

For example, the interior of our newest Akron-campus building, the seven-story Kay Jewelers Pavilion, was inspired by a child's natural play environment and purposely designed with children as our advisors to promote healing in a bright, comfortable space.

So, what are some of the lessons and strategies you will find in these pages? Note that in the table of contents, the chapters spell out the word *leadership*. A gimmick? Perhaps, but I've found when I use this device at presentations the message is well-received, easy to remember, and serves as a ready reference to track your success as a leader.

We'll also revisit Angie, her family, and some of the other miracle children I've been privileged to know. They have much to teach us, and at Akron Children's we have learned to listen carefully.

Remember Angie's casual take on chemo and radiation? "No time for bad hair days." That's your first lesson: Focus on substance, not style. Deal with what's important immediately because time is short for you to make a difference. As a leader, you must be a suncatcher. We'll discuss this more fully in a later chapter.

Angie's time with us was too short. But this remarkable child taught me a final lesson, directly related to what it means to be a values-infused organization. When she died at age 13, she left behind two unfinished suncatchers. One hangs in my office, a constant reminder that our work will never be done.

Leadership advice doesn't get any more practical than that.

William Considine
President and CEO
Akron Children's Hospital
May 2017

Bill Considine, 2016

1

LEADERSHIP

"Management is doing things right; leadership is doing the right things."

—Peter Drucker

When did you first come across the word *leadership*? I'm not sure when I first heard that word and tried to come to terms with its concept.

It could have been a word my kindergarten teacher used to help her students get a good start in education. Maybe it was my Cub Scout den mother, a Boy Scout scoutmaster, or something I picked up as an altar boy at St. Mary's Catholic Church from Monsignor Price or Sister James Ann. No doubt my Catholic Youth Organization coaches referred to leadership in our pregame pep talks.

I witnessed leadership at a very early age from my parents and numerous others who became my role models. Mom and Dad led several church and nonprofit groups. Their actions embodied the concept of servant leadership, and they involved the entire family.

Leadership became a more formal discussion in Junior Achievement class, during my student government days at

Archbishop Hoban High School, on the soccer team at The University of Akron, and interacting as student government president with Dr. Norman Auburn, former President of The University of Akron.

My graduate school experience brought a clearer focus on many of the aspects of leadership. That's when I began trying to define the word for myself.

SOME TYPES OF LEADERSHIP

There are different ways to think of leadership. It is a mistake to think leadership is only for those with titles—CEO, board chair, team captain, head nurse, or even admiral or general. Leadership exists—and is crucial—at all levels of an organization.

A few examples of leadership types include:

Servant leadership: These leaders are valuable to any organization and might even include volunteers as well as full-time employees. They don't wait for a leader to tell them what is needed. They sacrifice—often without notice or recognition—for the good of the organization. They act and get things done.

Leading with ideas: In many settings we look up to the smartest kid in the room, with good reason. Think of smart, creative people like Bill Gates and Steve Jobs. They might have dropped out of college, but they led a technological revolution that changed the way we interact and do business. (Just beware of strong personalities with bad ideas.)

Leading by experience: Many top leaders worked their way up through the ranks. What you learn along the way can give you the credentials and legitimacy to lead a department or major corporation, but just knowing the technical side of an enterprise is no guarantee you can lead people.

Leading by example: This type of leadership has always seemed to be the purest. As the situation dictates, real leaders rise to the top. Remember, titles don't always matter. Obvious examples would be military leaders or, to a lesser extent, sports figures. If leaders don't rise to the occasion under extreme stress, the entire organization is in trouble.

Look at these leadership categories, and feel free to add your own. You'll recognize the examples at all levels of your organization.

At Akron Children's Hospital, we depend on our staff to lead with high levels of service, with ideas on improvements, with their experience, and always by example.

My other source of leadership acumen comes from our patients—our miracle children—and their families. They show us how to handle stress with dignity. They often devote themselves to helping others, even during crises of their own. They give back by raising funds for research and donating their time in service to others. They help their healers heal.

You will see examples throughout this book as a reminder that leaders have to focus on what is essential. You also may discover inspiration where you least expect it.

LEARNING LEADERSHIP

Some people are natural leaders. Others learn by following best-leadership practices. All of us can refine our techniques and become more efficient in our thinking. We should learn to use a blend of leadership techniques, adding tools along the way and learning what to pull out of our toolboxes as needed.

Recruitment brochures for our country's military academies or U.S. Army Officer Candidate School list the requirements needed for leading men and women. One important trait is: "You must want to be a leader."

Who, you might think, doesn't want to lead? The answer is not that obvious. Leading requires self-sacrifice. You take heat from others who disagree with you. Good leaders spread the credit around but must absorb any blame. You're not one of the guys or girls anymore. You make tough decisions that have consequences. Again, think of the extreme example of a military setting.

In addition, you must promote fairness, diversity, and high ideals for all of your followers. Many people find it much more comfortable and safe to simply follow orders from someone else.

But if you're reading this book, you want to be a leader. Perhaps you've already started down that road and want to improve your skills or measure them against best practices. I hope what I have learned will give you some of the information you need.

Reflecting on my 45-year career in healthcare as well as on observations drawn from my lifelong journey, I've developed a leadership perspective based on these experiences. I've also read numerous leadership-themed books by people such as Peter Drucker, Stephen Covey, Jack Welch, and others.

I'm sure you've also found similar sources. Perhaps, like me, you keep asking, "But what does it all mean? How do I put leadership into practice?"

DEFINING LEADERSHIP

One thing that helped me was the launch of Akron Children's Hospital's Leadership Academy. This program was created to prepare people in our organization for taking leadership roles.

I took part in the first class as both participant and instructor. I was asked to help format the curriculum, specifically, to put in writing a definition of *leadership*.

Employees attending an Akron Children's Hospital Leadership Academy session.

Even after practicing leadership for decades, my initial response was a simple truth: "You'll know leadership when you see it in action."

Obviously, this statement was not much help for those trying to learn leadership techniques, so I was forced to focus on creating a short, workable definition for my organization. Here is what I came up with:

> *Leadership at Akron Children's embraces our heritage and tradition with a focus on service above self. Leadership captures being a role model, projecting a positive attitude, as well as being*

*respectful, trustworthy, humble, caring, fair, and
responsible through your every action.*

Bill Considine shares his thoughts on what it means to be a leader with
Leadership Academy attendees.

This definition won't work for all organizations, but it is worth
your time to come up with your own definition, either for your
organization, or better, for what your organization should be.
This will not only help bring into focus your leadership values
but will also make you consider the type of organization you
want to build, work for, or lead.

Akron Children's Leadership Academy continued teaching
me lessons. As I prepared a presentation for the academy, I re-
called a talk I gave several years earlier to a Leadership Akron
class. Leadership Akron is a program that equips people for
community involvement and leadership through an intensive
study of community issues and interactions with top decision
makers.

I thought I was going to talk about healthcare and prepared for that topic. When I arrived at the conference, I saw the title of my talk was "Leadership: What Is It?" This seemed a perfect time to share with the group a system I developed to remind myself of the traits that define the privileged leadership role.

BREAKING DOWN LEADERSHIP LESSONS

The device I use is to assign two concepts to each letter in the word *leadership*. These words are on a memory card in my mind, and I review them regularly. Here are my words:

L—Listen, Learn

E—Earn, Empower

A—Actions, Attitude

D—Dream, Dedication

E—Energy, Excitement

R—Respect, Role Modeling

S—Storyteller, Service

H—Humility, Humor

I—Improvement, Intellectual Independence

P—Privilege, People

Feel free to choose your own words and concepts, and add more as you progress on your leadership journey. You'll also find these concepts often overlap and reinforce each other.

In the following pages, I will discuss each word relationship and illustrate how the explanations bring leadership into action.

As noted, I've used this gimmick in presentations around the world to different types of groups and leadership levels. It has been extremely well-received as a learning device. More importantly, it helps me keep on track every day as the leader of a values-based organization.

In the next chapters, we'll work through the process in more detail.

DIGGING DEEPER—SELF-STUDY

- Think about when you became aware of leadership as a concept.
- What types of leadership most appeal to you?
- Who are your gurus of leadership? Where did you find them?

2

LISTEN, LEARN

"When people talk, listen completely."

—Ernest Hemingway

LISTEN

My mom often told my siblings and me that we needed to "just be quiet and listen and learn." Listening and learning go together.

As leaders, we have opportunities every day to listen to individuals who look to us for assistance. With that information there is knowledge to be gained that can expand our ability to develop effective facilitation skills. Leaders need to connect with people, and good listening skills are key to developing respectful, trustworthy relationships.

There is a memorial plaza at Kent State University to remember the four students killed on campus during the 1970 war protests. At the entrance to the plaza, a stone carving contains the words: "Inquire, Learn, Reflect."

These three words are shorthand for the scientific/academic method. We inquire about an issue (listening is a form of inquiry), we learn all we can, then we reflect or come to a solution.

This process provides a handy outline for making informed leadership decisions.

Listening is crucial for leaders. We are the ones who need to understand the people we come in contact with. We must be in the moment and focused on those individuals and groups. When you can place yourself in the moment, people sense they have your attention and are more comfortable sharing information.

Connecting through Listening

How do people know you are listening? Through:

- Good eye contact
- Open, positive body language
- Giving appreciative feedback
- Following up on the conversation
- Focusing on others, not yourself

It is important to filter information and not become a victim of what you hear—neither too defensive, nor flattered. Politely listen, then on your own time assess the information, learn from the input, think through the next steps, and react through follow-up actions.

Inquire, Learn, Reflect.

Practice these listening and assessment techniques until they become a natural part of your communication DNA.

Leaders who truly listen build credibility, show respect, create trusting relationships, engage and empower constituents, and increase their overall effectiveness. As noted earlier, when we listen, we learn.

Remember Angie from the introduction to this book? During her long stays with us, Akron Children's became a second home for her family. Her parents were thankful for our efforts, but they told me we could improve our support system for families in crisis.

"We think you need some kind of hospital advisory board," Angie's mother, Joyce, told me, "made up of parents affected by their children's illnesses. We see things you probably don't."

We listened and acted on her suggestion. Now, an important contributor to our hospital is the Parent Advisor Program. Volunteer parent advisors provide invaluable input on issues that impact our patients' care and represent their families' voices, as we work together to enhance how we deliver family-centered care.

A good example of this program in action is our Parent Mentor Program, which connects parents with other parents who have similar medical experiences. Parent mentors provide emotional support and information to parents and caregivers of children with special healthcare needs or disabilities. More than 100 volunteer mentors reach out to help families deal with a child's illness.

An Extra Sense

Some leaders practice a technique popularized in the 1980s, the concept of managing by walking around. Steve Jobs as well as Bill Hewlett and David Packard made great use of this management technique by walking around their workplaces to talk to their workers. The benefit of this approach to leadership, especially in today's world, is that you are visible and have the opportunity to listen with more than your ears.

Leaders I've admired over the years possessed the ability to listen with their eyes, their hearts, and through their respect for others. They had a sixth sense, capable of hearing and processing nonverbal messages from individuals and entire organizations.

Great leaders develop this super power. It complements the continuous learning that gives you credibility with your constituents.

You learn to be silent so you can hear the pulse of an organization as you walk the halls. You see the feedback from your audience. You feel the anxiety, pain, and joy of people through your openness and connection with them. You make a heart-to-heart connection.

Here in Akron, a priest by the name of Father Norm Douglas started an organization by that name: Heart to Heart Communications (H2HC). H2HC works with nonprofit groups to develop leaders "who want to make a difference."

What makes Father Norm's system unique is that H2HC's training focuses not just on developing leaders but on promoting the inner growth and development of employees, which is one of the keys to success for any organization.

Listening/learning is a continuous process. In the dynamics of leadership roles, what we learn assists greatly in empowering individuals. There is always more to learn about any issue, and it is especially important to listen to the perspective of those involved or affected.

I can still hear Mom saying, "Listen and learn." It is the foundation of any leadership strategy.

We have all seen examples of leaders who don't know their audience, are not present in the moment, fail to listen before they react, and/or haven't learned from their experiences. Here is one of my war stories.

Learning from Bad Examples

I once knew a very gifted, smart individual who held a respected leadership position and had a prestigious career, but he struggled with basic listening skills. When dealing with those reporting directly to him, he violated essential elements of respectful leadership.

He believed that no one was busier than him. His time had the most value. Scheduled meetings with him rarely started on time. When you did meet, he would sit at his desk and open mail as you discussed issues he supposedly wanted to understand. This was before the cellphone era, but he would accept calls during one-on-one meetings and even make calls while people were in his office, routinely turning his back on subordinates while talking.

Of course, later, he would question his staff on why he wasn't aware of an issue that had been discussed while he was preoccupied.

To many of you, this example might be familiar.

This leader violated many leadership principles, beginning with the most basic—listening. To their credit, his talented staff learned to work around his eccentricities. Each one, however, vowed to become a different type of leader when given the opportunity.

The lesson here: You often learn more from a bad experience with bad bosses, bad coaches, bad teachers, bad relationships. You see and feel firsthand what it's like to be disrespected, managed by fear or inattention, and subject to the whims of one who lacks proper dedication.

Remember these experiences and modify your leadership style to be positive, respectful, interactive, and proactive.

Inquire, Learn, Reflect.

Or use the STAR technique—Stop, Think, Assess, React—from Michael J. Termini's book *Walking the Talk: Moving into Leadership*.

And always thank people for sharing information, especially if the topic is unpleasant.

LEARN

> *"Leadership and learning are indispensable to each other."*
>
> —John F. Kennedy

It's been said that you don't know anything you've not learned from someone else. But you can only go so far on teaching—especially lessons that involve just lectures on subjects, including leadership. Don't think of learning from others merely as a product of the lecture hall or PowerPoint presentation.

Learning is active. Real learning is participatory, in which you are constantly questioning, evaluating, and testing the information you receive. True leaders are continuous learners and readily admit what they don't know.

We've all encountered know-it-all individuals. They enjoy listening to their own voices, are not good listeners and quickly lose the respect of people. What they really lose is the mantle of leadership, or their legitimacy to lead.

When Akron Children's started planning our $180 million Kay Jewelers Pavilion, we engaged national experts to design the new building. We also sought input from the staff members who would work there and asked for help from our patients, the children we serve.

The pavilion would house an updated, expanded neonatal intensive care unit (NICU), emergency department, outpatient surgery center, and special delivery unit for high-risk newborns.

With the general building design in hand, we took a team of doctors, nurses, technicians, patients, and families to an off-site facility where they could try out the spaces we were going to build.

A bright, welcoming space greets visitors to the Murdough Family Lobby in the Kay Jewelers Pavilion on the hospital's Akron campus.

Our staff and patient families could move around in full-size, cardboard mock-ups of rooms complete with operating tables, incubators, beds, medical technology units, controls, and family areas. If the designs were cumbersome or inefficient, we knew the time to find out was before they became permanent fixtures in the finished structure.

Many improvements were made based on the recommendations from our staff and families.

Of course, the children involved had their own ideas. So this high-tech space was built based on a backyard theme that reflects the joys of childhood and creates a comfortable environment for children and their families.

Families and staff evaluate the ease of flow through the proposed design of the new Kay Jewelers Pavilion.

The NICU, for instance, is The Treehouse, offering a soothing, healing space for families with babies requiring highly specialized care. Other themes include The Sandbox (outpatient surgery), The Puddle (ER), and The Garden (labor, delivery, and recovery center). Children's artwork adorns the hallways, and interactive video stations give patients and their siblings fun activities to help pass their time away from home.

We knew the technology we needed for our new building, but the final design was not complete until it worked for the children. We learned to see the world through the eyes of a child to serve our families better.

Sharing Leadership

All of us have an opportunity every day to learn from others and from life—both good and bad lessons. Leaders create an environment for individuals to share their experiences and learn from each other.

In the book *All I Really Need to Know I Learned in Kindergarten*, Robert Fulghum pared down the key to future success: sharing. Sharing is critical.

True leaders share throughout their organizations: information, credit, decision making.

Leaders who embrace continuous learning for themselves should also promote that philosophy for others and allow them to share the benefits. Leaders should implement career development plans for their direct reports, for instance, and allow those shared values to filter out from the top.

Organizational leadership training, tuition assistance programs, career or life coaches, mentors, manpower planning, wellness programs, and more promote the importance of lifelong learning. These kinds of nonthreatening learning opportunities help improve individuals and organizations.

What is the most obvious asset to leaders? Surround yourself with the best possible people. Leaders who celebrate learning and make it a priority attract, develop, and keep the best employees and administrators.

DIGGING DEEPER—SELF-STUDY

- Find ways to actively work on your listening skills.
- Develop your own take on "Inquire, Learn, Reflect."
- Consciously try to avoid being the boss others cite as a bad example of listening and learning.
- Seek out nontraditional sources for input on organizational decisions.

3

EARN, EMPOWER

> *"Whatever affects one directly, affects all indirectly.
> I can never be what I ought to be until you are what
> you ought to be."*
>
> —Dr. Martin Luther King Jr.

EARN

We are all familiar with the phrase "You have to earn your stripes."

True leadership is a role you need to earn. Titles have their value and often provide clarity about a person's place in the organizational structure. Leadership, however, is not guaranteed by a title. Neither, necessarily, is respect.

Being CEO of a children's hospital can be humbling in that regard. You can't fool children, especially ill children who have a more direct connection with life than most adults.

Out of the Comfort Zone

Ridge had been a patient at Akron Children's almost since his birth. He once approached me in the hallway while he was collecting donations for an early Christmas party in his area.

Ready to help out, I rattled a quarter into his canister. Ridge looked up and said, "Don't you have any dollars?"

Now, I've been approached by sophisticated fund-raisers who said basically the same thing. But they took a less direct route when asking for my money. Ridge was not impressed by my title, and he was in a hurry to complete his mission. Remember, sick children don't have time for bad hair days—or nuance.

The lesson here is that you must be worthy of the respect of your peers and

"Change bandit" Ridge Miller

others. If you—in their minds—somehow shortchange them, they might not be honest with you about their feelings, and you will have missed a chance to earn their loyalty. Leaders can't allow such chances to go unrealized.

The most effective leaders earned that privileged mantle through their actions, beliefs, values, performance, and behavior.

Leaders Without Titles

There are numerous examples of people in organizations who have influence and are viewed as "leaders without titles." They set the tone, either good or bad, and are expected by others to take the lead on any issue that arises.

In your own relationships, whom do you consider a leader and why? Who are the most effective leaders you know, and in your experience what individuals were expected to lead because they had a title yet failed?

This is when we might look at old war movies for an example. One common plot device tells the story of a general's favorite soldier being given a title or rank, but another soldier comes out of nowhere, showing true leadership when the pressure is on.

This is reflected in a quote by Peter Drucker: "Rank does not confer privilege or give power; it imposes responsibility."

You don't have to be in a life-or-death situation to recognize responsible leadership in action. Any organizational crisis—or even deadline—proves that leadership must be earned; not given because of money, power, well-placed friends, family ties, or other reasons.

Often leadership is awarded because an individual has exceptional talent in an area of specialty. But these skills have little to do with the responsibilities of leadership. Great writers may not make great editors. Great doctors don't necessarily make great administrators.

Individuals can be coached, however, and occasionally meld quickly into the leader's role. But they often are under intense scrutiny to perform and earn the respect that comes with the title.

So you have to earn leadership daily in your every action. Otherwise, like me being approached by young Ridge, you can be made to feel uncomfortable when confronted by someone else's reality.

People like Ridge are what I call "change bandits." You can learn a lot from them.

Setting the Right Tone

Remember, you are the standard-bearer. You set the tone. We all are accustomed to earning a grade, medal, merit badge, respect, degree, spot on the team, and more. We understand there is a right way and wrong way to earn these achievements—and deserve them.

The same applies to leadership. It must be earned through being:

Prepared

Honest

Humble

Caring

Trustworthy

Responsible

Inclusive

Fair

You should take this list and add the character traits that you think make a true leader. Which ones do you need to work on?

You earn your mantle of leadership by giving service to others and having a relentless drive to make a positive difference in people's lives, especially the people who look up to you.

Leader as Servant

I left a few things out in the story a few pages back about our young friend and patient, Ridge, who was collecting money for a Christmas party. The cause is significant because Ridge spent every Christmas of his four short years at Akron Children's Hospital.

He came to us before he was one year old and went through multiple treatments for several diseases. Ridge grew up at Akron Children's, and his loss was felt by everyone who came in contact with him.

Curiously, Ridge's funeral was an uplifting ceremony. He was surrounded by his favorite, most comforting possessions. He was wearing SpongeBob SquarePants pajamas, covered by a SpongeBob quilt. The casket was decorated as a train, and his headstone also was train-shaped. It was not a time for sadness his mother, Donna, told me because Ridge had a "wonderful life."

"From the day he was born until the day he died, Ridge knew only love," Donna said. "Everyone gave him their best every day, and when he got older he returned the love in bushel baskets."

If you want to earn your place as a trusted leader, give more than you take and let your actions reflect a philosophy of service and caring.

DIGGING DEEPER—SELF-STUDY

- Look around you for leaders without titles—what characteristics do they possess?
- Seek out examples of servant leadership in your organization. What does it look like?
- Think of a time you were out of your comfort zone. What did you learn?

EMPOWER

"Don't tell people how to do things. Tell them what to do and let them surprise you with their results."

—George S. Patton Jr.

One characteristic of a great leader is the ability to empower others and get them to believe in a core vision and their own capabilities.

One of my earliest and most influential mentors was a man named John Danielson. I worked for him at Memorial Hospital, the teaching institution for the University of North Carolina, in Chapel Hill.

The Hows and Whys of Empowerment

Danielson was a master of empowerment. I would seek his advice on many issues and problems that crossed my desk. At first I found it frustrating that he would listen yet rarely offer any solutions. To the contrary, he would solicit my ideas, provide encouragement, gently push me out of my comfort zone, and show enormous belief in my abilities.

In each instance, I would leave his office with more confidence in my instincts and a sense of legitimacy for my decisions.

In turn, Danielson let everyone in the organization know that he valued my ideas. He never second-guessed a decision. When I made a wrong or incomplete decision on a course of action, he provided coaching to marshal support, celebrated lessons learned, and got the issue back on track.

Leaders empower others.

Other examples of such empowerment are all around us. Permit me another movie reference.

Mentor and Coaches

In *Remember the Titans*, the star quarterback is tackled when a teammate misses an assignment on purpose. The quarterback suffers a broken wrist.

It is a critical game, and Coach Boone, played by Denzel Washington, turns to his backup quarterback, Ronnie Bass.

The coach immediately empowers Ronnie to step up and be the leader his team needs. He shares a quick story with Ronnie, a new California kid nicknamed "Sunshine."

Ronnie doesn't think he can replace the injured quarterback, so Coach Boone tells Ronnie a story. When he was 15 years old, his mother and father both died—in the same month. The coach was the youngest of 12 siblings, "all looking up to me."

"Now, I wasn't ready yet, either, but they needed me," Boone said. "Your team needs you tonight. ... You're going to command your troops."

Ronnie's doubts dissolve and, with the magic of Hollywood, he leads the team to victory and is awarded the game ball. The coach's confidence in his player was the key to Ronnie's development.

John Danielson gave me a similar gift, and no doubt you have mentors who do the same. If not, look for a mentor who will push you to be your best.

The Power of Belief

Belief, including self-belief, is a constant theme in leadership.

At Akron Children's, we see this power demonstrated almost daily in our miracle children. Abby, for instance, was a gifted student and soccer player at a local college. She was always tired and, after numerous tests, was diagnosed with a rare cancer.

Her medical care was supplemented by the lessons she learned from sports and life. Her

Abigail Hexamer

self-treatment included fortitude, positive energy, and a mind-over-matter plan to beat cancer.

Abby was so successful that we asked her to be a spokesperson for the hospital on the power of belief.

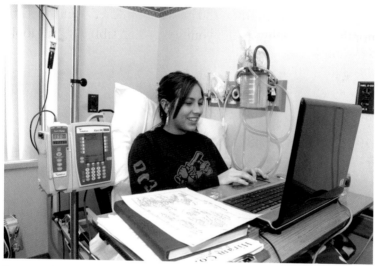

Lessons learned from sports about staying positive saw Abby through her battle with cancer.

Another movie that highlights the importance in believing (okay, I watch a lot of movies) is *The Polar Express*.

This movie wraps up on Christmas morning, after a young boy, Hero Boy, completes a Christmas dream adventure and opens his last, but very special, Christmas gift.

The gift is the bell from the reindeer harness on Santa's sleigh, which he had received as "the first gift of Christmas." It had a beautiful ring and bright reflection, but Hero Boy thought he had lost the bell during his adventure through a hole in the pocket of his robe.

His parents could not hear the ring of the bell because they did not believe. His sister could hear the remarkable ring yet, over time, she lost the ability to hear it.

Only the young boy was empowered to keep believing. The narrator ends the story by saying the bell only rings for those who truly believe.

The bell still rings for Hero Boy today.

Abby and other miracle kids hear the bell.

Mr. Danielson gave me the opportunity to hear the bell ring and empowered me to believe in myself. That belief and the enriching sound of the bell still provide me with inner peace.

Leaders empower others, and that empowerment leads to belief.

DIGGING DEEPER—SELF-STUDY

- Have you ever been empowered by a mentor, or have you empowered others? What lessons did you learn?
- Have you experienced the power of belief (not necessarily in the religious sense)?
- How can you cultivate that power?

4

ACTION, ATTITUDE

"Action is the foundational key to all success."

—Pablo Picasso

ACTION

I can't emphasize enough that leadership is what you do—not who you know or who you are.

Outstanding leaders are known for being action-oriented. They possess a can-do attitude and understand the need to involve people and empower them to act. Leaders are not change-for-change's-sake people. They are not couch potatoes or we've-never-done-it-that-way people.

Leaders know the status quo can be a dangerous comfort zone. Action keeps people involved.

The Perils of Inaction

"There are risks and costs to a program of action," John F. Kennedy once noted. "But they are far less than the long-range risks of comfortable inaction."

Let's revisit our military model. In combat, a wrong decision often is better than no decision. A wrong or risky decision at least sets a course of action in motion and forces the issue. It can reveal, even mid-course, the correct adjustment needed for victory.

During the Civil War battle for Gettysburg, the Union's far-left flank was defended by the 20th Maine regiment, under the command of a former Bowdoin College professor, Col. Joshua Chamberlain. The Maine soldiers held the critical point on Little Round Top, which if lost could mean retreat for the entire Union line.

After two hours of repeated attacks from an Alabama brigade, Chamberlain's unit had lost a third of its men and was out of ammunition. Facing what they thought would be the final assault, Chamberlain did the unexpected. He ordered a bayonet charge against the attacking force.

If he had asked his superiors—or consulted a military manual—Chamberlain would have found little support for attacking from a defensive, hilltop position. But the audacity of the charge stopped the superior enemy force, which surrendered to the Maine troops. Chamberlain won arguably the decisive skirmish of the war's decisive battle.

I'm not advocating for wrong decisions. But often a calculated risk can carry the day over inaction, especially when compared to doing things the way they have always been done.

The Healthy Organization

Inaction can be frustrating in any organization, and it dampens the innovative spirit so essential to success. At Akron Children's Hospital, we don't have to look far to see direct evidence of this. When illness strikes, inaction can literally kill.

Our medical staff makes life-and-death decisions so often they become second nature. Once a course of action, or treatment, is begun, it can be adjusted to fit changing conditions. The more hazardous course would be to do nothing.

With obvious differences, this holds true for any organization.

Remember John Danielson, my valued mentor from the last chapter? Danielson often referred to an organization, such as our hospital, as a biological, anatomical entity. In other words, a hospital is like a patient. It can get sick, tired, or otherwise find itself in less-than-peak health.

Danielson knew that one major cause of sickness was inaction relative to a needed decision. Absent action, he said, the organization becomes constipated. It's a graphic image but illustrates the dull, weakened state of functioning at reduced capacity.

Shortly after he hired me, Danielson introduced me as a new member of his team. To emphasize my role in an easy-to-understand way, he said the hospital was feeling constipated, and I was the "Ex-Lax pill."

Danielson expected me to take action, make decisions, involve people, and get the system moving again. Continuing his memorable scenario, he said that, although the action could be a mess at first, he knew we would all feel better soon.

Now, I'm not recommending you refer to your team as Ex-Lax pills. I am suggesting that you, as a leader, understand the importance of promoting action as the solution to a sluggish organization.

"Fresh activity," said Johann Wolfgang von Goethe, "is the only means of overcoming adversity."

You will, through your actions, gain credibility and confidence from those who look to you for direction. Be a doer who involves, empowers, and celebrates with your people.

The old phrase "Actions speak louder than words," is very true, especially when applied to creating a culture of continuous improvement and establishing yourself as the leader of a rich organizational culture.

As Thomas Jefferson said, "Do you want to know who you are? Don't ask. Act! Action will delineate and define you."

DIGGING DEEPER—SELF-STUDY

- If your organization were a biological entity, how healthy would it be?
- List several points of "illness" or "constipation" that require action.
- Think about how you can be the catalyst for such action.

ATTITUDE

"Whether you think you can, or you think you can't—you're right."

—Henry Ford

My mother, probably like yours, reminded me routinely to "get my attitude straight." A glass half full was always better than a glass half empty.

In college I knew a football coach who promoted positive mental attitude (PMA) in every phase of his life, teaching, and coaching. All of his students, assistant coaches, recruits, players, and even family members were influenced by this philosophy.

Decades later, Coach Jim Dennison is still admired because his every action embraced a positive attitude. No one ever wins the blame game. A PMA approach from a leader can bring the best effort from his or her team and show them their potential.

A Leader's Attitude

A positive attitude is a leader's attitude. Leaders such as Coach Dennison set the tone and provide excitement, creativity, opportunities, and top performances. In your progress as a leader, you must cultivate this attitude.

Attitude is key to an organization's culture and essential to empower those around you. We've all seen examples of how a positive, can-do attitude can invite innovation and promote respect among any team in any setting.

Attitude encourages a just culture, as individuals deal transparently with each other and take responsibility for their actions. Attitude acknowledges and respects history and tradition, not by living in the past but by building on the foundations that have true values and beliefs.

Again, using military and sports metaphors, we can find direct lessons on performing under pressure situations. In sports, team leaders must overcome a bad call, fumble, foul, or other bad break that threatens the outcome of a game. And sometimes, the bad break involves more than the game.

One important sports figure from the last few decades is Jim Valvano, whose North Carolina State team came from nowhere to win the 1983 NCAA men's basketball championship. But that was just the start of Coach Valvano's legacy.

He fought a very visible and ultimately losing battle with cancer. He spent his final months using his fame to speak out on the need for cancer research and to encourage cancer victims. His oft-quoted mantra was, "Don't give up. Don't ever give up."

He and ESPN founded the V Foundation for Cancer Research. The Jimmy V Classic college basketball tournament raises millions each year to fight cancer.

> *"I love to win, but I love to lose almost as much. I love the thrill of victory, and I also love the challenge of defeat."*
>
> —Lou Gehrig

Frontline Heroes

Remember our patient Angie and her suncatchers? Sometimes attitude becomes your legacy. We can learn many lessons from sports, but my heroes when it comes to attitude are found at Akron Children's Hospital. In fact, I could write an entire book about the lessons I've learned from our miracle children.

Their stories inspire my own attitude. You recall Abby from the last chapter, a college athlete who came through cancer to speak for the hospital on the power of belief.

Caleb Thurman

There is also Caleb, a local honor student, who wears leg braces but competes on his high school's wrestling and base-ball teams. "The right attitude," he says, "is so important."

But one special girl comes to mind when I speak of attitude. Cassidy had dreams of becoming an artist. The 11-year-old was admitted to our palliative care unit so we could manage the care for her chronic, life-threatening conditions.

Palliative care to Cassidy became the Palette of Care, a concept embraced by our staff because it perfectly describes the range of transdisciplinary care offered to the most seriously ill children.

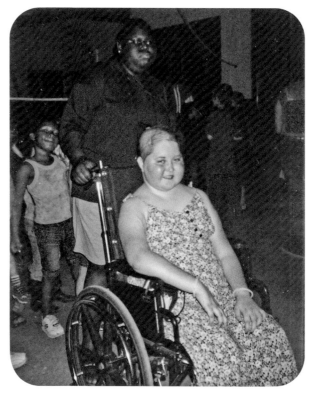

Cassidy Jackson

This is the concept Cassidy set to art. She painted a beautiful picture of her vision of the Palette of Care—a palm tree and sunshine bathed in a wealth of color. She painted with talent, heart, and attitude. Surgery and treatment had left the right side of her body paralyzed. No matter. She painted with her left hand.

Cassidy's Palette of Care

The hospital copyrighted her artwork and trademarked "Palette of Care" for this important department. Cassidy is gone now, but her art and spirit will always be with us.

This leadership essential, attitude, is always close by for me. Our children and their families are fighting on the front lines of life. They see action every day. It takes great courage to keep fighting when there is no guarantee of a successful result.

There are no rainouts with cancer, no do-overs for birth defects. Our patients and their families start where they are and carry on bravely from there. When I think of attitude, these are my teachers and real-life heroes.

DIGGING DEEPER—SELF-STUDY

- Does your culture support a positive attitude throughout the ranks?

- Think about a time when you succeeded on an issue or problem simply by refusing to give up or give in. What did you learn that could apply to other situations?

- How do you develop your own "leader's attitude?"

5

DREAM, DEDICATION

"The future belongs to those who believe in the beauty of their dreams."

—Eleanor Roosevelt

DREAM

The ability to make the impossible possible and the improbable probable are attributes of leadership. Leaders dream and know how to make their dreams come true.

The best leaders are known as visionaries. They have the ability to share a dream with others and create excitement about new possibilities. Leaders move beyond the status quo with dreams that empower, excite, and create a better alternative for all involved.

I grew up in an era of great national leaders who knew how to share their dreams. President John F. Kennedy and Dr. Martin Luther King Jr. routinely challenged the status quo and shared their dreams with the whole world.

Have a Dream

Dr. King's "I Have a Dream" speech galvanized the nation around the possibilities of national equality and diversity of opportunity. His dreams did no less than change the face of America and the way Americans think about each other.

Kennedy also had a dream of a more inclusive, innovative society—a dream that involved and electrified the young men and women of our country. His dream envisioned the discovery of new worlds through space exploration and tackling world problems through volunteer service. His dreams became reality with the creation of the Peace Corps and the expansion of the space program, and they promoted a sense of personal responsibility among a new generation.

In his inaugural address, Kennedy famously challenged Americans to "ask not what your country can do for you, ask what you can do for your country." That sentiment reached the ears and hearts of millions. Kennedy inspired people to get involved in public service in their communities and beyond, to tackle social justice issues and undertake scientific adventure.

President Kennedy's announcement in 1962 of his plan for a manned, round-trip flight to the moon by the end of the decade was a challenge as well as a vision. He noted that we choose to go to the moon "not because it is easy but because it is hard."

The challenge was for America to come together in a great common purpose, a peaceful mission that would engage our best minds, talent, and technology.

The resulting moon mission paid great dividends to the world, through advancements in science, medical research, technology, and human possibilities.

Communicate the Dream

The dream element in leadership depends on communication. Kennedy, as well as Dr. King, communicated their lofty goals and created the belief that we, as a team, could reach and surpass the impossible.

Kennedy truly offered hope through his leadership to the disenfranchised youth of our country at a time of great anxiety and uncertainty. His determined, calm, decisive approach, along with his forward-looking dreams, formed the perfect platform for leadership.

King also knew that dreams are a form of hope. He gave hope to minorities and all Americans—for generations to come—that we can solve the most pressing problems if we work together.

Such leaders on a national level come along only once in a generation, if we are lucky. We need such leadership today, along with a moon-launch-type effort to address a new generation of problems—rebuilding our infrastructure, shrinking poverty, and lifting education to higher standards.

Kennedy, King, and other great leaders are more than visionaries. They brought real-life experience to their vision by sharing a dream that all people could identify with and get excited about.

Eleanor Roosevelt sums up this wisdom: "To handle yourself, use your head; to handle others, use your heart."

Tell Your Story

Great leaders mix storytelling with their dreams. They communicate the possibilities and illuminate the path to achieve those possibilities. Individuals want to follow these leaders because their dreams offer a better way, and they accept the work necessary to fulfill them.

One of our miracle kids at Akron Children's Hospital suffered from cerebral palsy and a host of other problems. Zack's dream was to help future children get the care they needed for similar ills. He was such a good spokesman for the hospital that we took him to Washington, D.C., to meet with legislative leaders and discuss legislation affecting children's healthcare—to tell his story.

Zack's sister, Megan, blogged about Zack and his activities. The media picked up Megan's stories, and Zack became a very effective voice on pediatric health issues.

Zack died on Christmas Eve more than a decade ago. But Megan has been keeping his dream alive and continues to communicate on his behalf. In fact, Megan attends The University of Akron's School of Nursing and serves as a student aide at our hospital.

Neither Zack, President Kennedy, nor Dr. King lived to see their dreams realized. But remember, the key to a leader's dream is having the ability to communicate the essence of the dream so it can become a reality. Great dreams excite others to carry on after the leader is gone.

DIGGING DEEPER—SELF-STUDY

- Think about your own dreams and how to make them a priority in your life.
- How can your dreams help your organization or the organization you want to build?
- How do you communicate your dreams to others?

DEDICATION

> *"We all have dreams. In order to make dreams come into reality, it takes an awful lot of determination, dedication, self-discipline and effort."*
>
> —Jesse Owens

Leadership requires raising your own performance and proving to others you are dedicated to the privileged leadership role.

You are now in a fish bowl, and people see very clearly your actions, work ethic, and dedication. A selfish leader will quickly lose people's trust. Those who depend on you can immediately assess whether your dedication is self-centered. If so, they will realize that they—and their needs—can be sacrificed at any moment.

Dedicated leaders understand they often must sacrifice their own schedule to make time to serve others. Dedicated leadership requires responding to others' schedules and needs—to always be available, approachable, and visible.

Applying Dedication to Leadership

Dedication means modeling the way forward, never having a bad hair day, and proving that you put your duties of leadership to others before self.

If you are not comfortable with this essential arrangement, you should revisit a passage from an earlier chapter and ask whether you really want to be a leader.

Dedicated leaders must go the extra mile. They get to know the people in their organizations. They care. They routinely send thank-you notes and notes of congratulations. They make appearances at events, ceremonies, funerals, and more.

Their dedication keeps them grounded and maintains that extra bond with the people who look to them for reassurance, direction, and empowerment.

Many times a leader must reassure others beyond employees. Good or bad news about an organization affects clients, patients, shareholders, and the public. At these times, a leader speaks for the organization, providing assurance in times of crisis but always communicating the spirit and values of the organization, as well as offering facts and solutions.

Handled properly, even a crisis can enhance an organization's reputation as well as that of the leader, who reflects the image and values of the institution.

Dedicated leaders are dependable. They welcome the chance to step up and take charge in good and bad situations. They show up, and you know they want to be there.

Always, they have time for you regardless of the pressures they may be under, and they don't make excuses. That dedication is seen and appreciated by all around them.

DIGGING DEEPER—SELF-STUDY

- Who are your model(s) of a dedicated leader?
- How have you incorporated her or his example into your own leadership growth?
- Sketch out three actions you can take immediately to make yourself a more dedicated leader.

6

ENERGY, EXCITE

"Energy, invincible determination with the right motive, are the levers that move the world."

—Noah Porter

ENERGY

Leaders naturally are expected to excite and energize people in their organizations.

There are numerous ways to create energy. The key is to exude positive energy that excites, empowers, and motivates your team.

We all have been in settings where an individual projects negative energy. This person is sullen and discouraging—a woe-is-me type. Nothing is ever good enough. There are no solutions. The sky is falling.

To their bosses, they complain about colleagues or those they supervise. They are lazy, do not follow instructions, or are poor performers. To other employees, they complain about their bosses or company. The parent company is out of touch, we don't get the resources we need, or upper management is incompetent.

Energy Vampires

Negative energy abounds. When we interact with these energy vampires, we become drained. An hour with them seems like a day; a day like a week. We simply get exhausted and avoid further interaction.

We don't need our workplace setting to see negativity in action. Think of a time when you were a customer in a supermarket, retail store, or theater and the employees were griping about their jobs or company. Is this the kind of business you want to patronize? Neither do I.

On the other hand, a leader who constantly brings positive energy to discussions and solicits input, promotes new beginnings, and celebrates opportunities, regardless of the challenge, rejuvenates a team.

Smiles appear on faces, stress levels drop, and team performance, productivity, and satisfaction all improve. People look forward to coming to work and interacting with these colleagues. Everyone knows his or her work is meaningful, noticed, and making a difference. The energy is positive, and people work as a team out of respect for the leaders, not out of fear of reprisal or blame.

Negativity is self-reinforcing, but so is positive energy. We can illustrate this concept with a sporting analogy. When sportscasters talk about a change in momentum, what they mean is they see the twin poles of energy, which either team can experience, change from positive to negative or vice versa.

A great play or series of plays can create a positive force for one side while the other experiences negative energy. This negativity can lead to a loss of confidence, resulting in the expectation that other things will go wrong. That often happens as the negativity piles up. The momentum shifts, and it can be difficult to get back.

It's the same in many organizational settings. Your job as a leader is to emit positive energy and keep momentum on your side.

DIGGING DEEPER—SELF-STUDY

- What is the energy level of your organization?
- How can you infuse your colleagues and those you lead with positive energy?
- Take one action today to reduce negativity in your organization. Take another action tomorrow.

EXCITE

> *"The greatest leader is not necessarily the one who does the greatest things. He is the one who gets the people to do the greatest things."*
>
> —Ronald Reagan

Leaders obviously must bring energy to their tasks and their organization's culture. As mentioned in an earlier chapter, they need to be adept at empowering people and bringing out each individual's full potential. It's imperative that leaders earn their mantle of leadership daily through their actions and values, especially by respecting the views of others.

With those elements in place, a leader's ability to excite others positively about opportunities produces a secret sauce that enables an organization's can-do attitude.

Remember Cassidy, the artist who designed our Palette of Care logo? She is a perfect example of someone with a can-do attitude under the most desperate circumstances. Such an attitude catches on and can excite an entire organization or enterprise.

A leader infuses excitement through language—both spoken and unspoken—to show the opportunity found in challenging situations. Again, people get excited about making the improbable probable, and the impossible possible.

It is up to leaders to excite people by finding the opportunity and clarity in ambiguity. Leaders excite their teams by being architects of change, not victims of change.

Said Margaret Wheatley, "The things we fear most in organizations—fluctuations, disturbances, imbalances—are the primary sources of creativity."

Embrace Change and Risk

Exciting people leads to innovative thought, risk-taking, cooperative learning, and working in a transparent environment as a team.

Change can be the canvas on which you do your best work.

Nowhere is change more constant than in the medical field. We take for granted that there will be constant change in medical techniques and technology, medicines and therapies, and training for professionals. We constantly deal with changes in the healthcare environment from insurance companies, government regulations, and the basic economics of the medical business.

Leaders in such an environment must develop the ability to excite but not alarm. This involves a management style that shows belief and trust in people, instead of managing through fear. An excited team looks forward to work and is willing to be innovative because they know the blame game is not the bottom line.

Like a basketball coach who tells his team to go out and make mistakes, a properly motivated workplace team embraces failure as a learning experience that will pay dividends in the next initiative.

Motivating people through honest communication creates the positive energy that leaders seek and provides an excitement that invigorates the entire culture. We think of excitement about possibilities as the medicine in the healthcare field. Excitement allows that positive mind-set. A belief that, "I can do this."

Mind over matter.

Expect Miracles

As CEO of a children's hospital I've seen many miracles of people beating the odds because they could generate a certain kind of excitement, of turning a negative into a positive.

Bill Considine and Trevor Weigand catch up at a basketball game.

One patient, Trevor, was a high school basketball player and son of a college coach. He had been through several surgeries for cancerous tumors. Rather than bemoan his fate, Trevor began organizing weekend basketball tournaments to raise money for Akron Children's Hospital.

People like Trevor don't talk about making a difference—they go out and do it. That's leadership.

Team Trevor presents a check to hospital staff.

One thing I have learned from such examples is that a CEO cannot be a phony and still excite the troops. Honesty is essential. As you deliver an honest message, you can be either a doomsday communicator or a positive-possibility person. You have a choice.

One of my mentors told me to remember people were watching me and listening to me through my words and also my actions. If my words and actions indicated that I had a cold, in a day or two the entire organization would have pneumonia.

You can excite people by being your organization's number one cheerleader and storyteller.

President John F. Kennedy excited my generation with his words and actions. He talked about space exploration, civil rights, empowering youth, and more. Which individuals in your life have had that excitement DNA in their management style? Does your own management style provide positive excitement?

DIGGING DEEPER—SELF-STUDY

- Does your organizational attitude embrace change?
- What vehicles do you have in place to communicate excitement within your organization?
- Think of a time you experienced stressful workplace change. What did you learn?

7

RESPECT, ROLE MODEL

"Treat people as if they were what they ought to be, and you help them become what they are capable of being."

—Johan Wolfgang van Goethe

RESPECT

Leaders who excel at leadership understand the art of showing respect.

We all know how it feels to be disrespected, marginalized, maligned, and more. Leaders I admire know those emotions and the negative effect this mind-set can have on an individual's or team's performance.

Tom Peters and Robert H. Waterman, authors of *In Search of Excellence*, did a study of America's best-run companies. They discovered that companies with the best performances emphasized values.

Those that focused only on financial objectives or ignored values completely didn't do as well. Why? The authors said that financial objectives might motivate the top 15 executives in a company or even the top 50.

"But those objectives alone seldom add much zest to life down the line," they wrote, "to the tens of thousands who make, sell and service the product."

Peters and Waterman were onto something very important. It would be naïve to suggest that financial incentives don't appeal to most people. Bonus programs, stock options, and even employee-ownership ventures are effective tools to capture people's attention and loyalty. Tying pay to performance is a proven methodology.

But listen to the phrase they use, "seldom add much zest to life." By zest they mean the collective elements that make life worth living—service to others, satisfaction in a job well done, basic human values.

Why is it important to take people beyond the mercenary approach of "you get this much money for this much effort"? And why even bother with motivating the "people down the line"?

Individual Acts

Frederick G. Harmon explains in his book *Playing for Keeps* that, "The small, individual act is the basic cell of all performance. Everything we call management ends there."

The people in an organization and the thousands of little acts they perform each day are the cells that make up an organization. If the actions are the best each day that those in your group can deliver, you will have an outstanding, high-quality organization. Conversely, if those actions are feeble, incomplete, or lackluster, so too will be the quality of the organization. Garbage in, garbage out, as the early computer programmers used to say.

What feeds those basic cells? What is at the heart of an organization?

I suggest the answer is *values*.

Values determine the quality of those thousands of little cells. This is true of large corporations, schools, social clubs, and even families.

The people in virtually all organizations are under stress, at least part of the time. As a leader, your job is to respect that condition and find what motivates top performance beyond a paycheck. Money alone doesn't provide the incentive for getting workers to go the extra mile for your company.

This reality is especially crucial to recognize in a nonprofit or service organization. At Akron Children's Hospital we are motivated by helping children and their families. There is a natural sense of mission among doctors, nurses, and staff. By helping others, we leave a lasting legacy.

How can you infuse that sense of mission in your organization? Look back to the metaphor of an organization as a living being. Just as a biological heart produces forces such as pressure, rhythm, and velocity, so too the invisible heart of an organization produces observable forces.

Vital Signs

I believe there are four signs of an organization's heart:

- Trust
- Purpose
- Beliefs
- Respect

In the next section, "Role Model," we'll discuss the leader's crucial role in maintaining an organization's heart health. But first, let's look at the four signs, beginning with *trust*.

Often when we think of trust and organizations, we think of the relationships between companies and customers. That type of trust is certainly critical to an organization's success, but it is an external type of trust. The trust that forms an organization's vital sign is internal.

James Autry covers this concept in his book *Love and Profit: The Art of Caring Leadership*. Autry says, "You as a manager must trust your employees to do their work. You must trust them almost beyond reason and let them know you believe what they say."

Autry also notes, "The manager who has overcome the fear of trust has taken a major step in getting the best results the group can produce."

Why? What is so empowering about trust?

Think of trust as the blood pressure of your organization. Trust carries energy to each cell, to each member. Every act of trust we place in our family or coworkers is an expression of confidence.

Trust is a compliment. It energizes people by adding to their sense of self-worth. Who doesn't swell a bit with pride when they are referred to as trustworthy?

The first time you hand over the keys to the family car to a 16-year-old son or daughter, you demonstrate your trust. You are saying, "I believe in you." By the way, I don't recommend doing a pulse check at that particular moment. Trust can be scary.

One example of trust that enables an organization to succeed is the relationship between a quarterback and his receivers. The quarterback throws the ball not to where his teammate is standing, but to the place he expects the receiver to be. He places trust in the receiver's ability to be there when the ball arrives, and the receiver expects the ball to be where he is going. They've practiced and developed trust in each other.

Over time, they have learned what the other is thinking and can accomplish more than they ever dreamed possible.

Stop and think for a moment. How many times yesterday did you take that kind of leap of faith with your family? How many times in your place of work were you willing to let go of the ball and trust your coworker to be there to catch it?

Is trust present in your organization? To find out, ask yourself: Are the people in your organization empowered?

Finding Purpose

The second vital sign of an organization's healthy heart is a *sense of purpose.*

In their book *The Soul at Work,* Roger Lewin and Birute Regine argue that the difference between machines and organizations can be found in the different spellings of the word *soul.* They say a machine has a sole purpose. An organization, however, has a *soul* purpose, and that, they say, is not about making money. It's about actualizing dreams of a higher purpose that serve a greater good.

Remember Peters and Waterman and their organizational studies? They say, "Excellent companies seem to understand that every man seeks meaning."

Their research found that the need for meaning is so strong most people will not only work harder but will surrender a fair degree of freedom to organizations that provide meaning. Financial incentives might work in the short term but if not tied to purpose, over time they only serve to accentuate the lack of purpose within an organization. That can lead to that company's demise.

At Akron Children's, we see this in our patients and families. They seek meaning in a child's illness and often find purpose in raising money, volunteering, or championing a special cause.

Human beings crave meaning in their lives. We seek it through religion, philosophy, and art. Isn't it obvious then, that people seek meaning in their organizations, particularly in the jobs where we spend most of our waking hours?

Purpose within an organization can be as simple as a desire to be the best at what you do or wanting to treat others the way you want to be treated. Our purpose can be broad or as focused as being a champion for children with Down syndrome.

There is nothing to limit the scope of an organization's purpose. In fact, broader is often better. For example, have you ever noticed the statement of purpose so neatly tucked into the Lord's Prayer?

For those of the Christian faith, what do you think it means when you say, "Thy kingdom come, thy will be done, on earth as it is in heaven?" From my perspective, that sure sounds like a statement of purpose, as well as a wonderful way to start the day.

Think about it. That simple sentence gives us:

- What we want—"Thy kingdom come"
- How we make it happen—"Thy will be done"
- And our individual responsibility for making it so—"On earth as it is in heaven."

Jim Collins, author of the popular management books *Good to Great* and *Built to Last* also touches on this theme in his three definitions of ultimate greatness for organizations.

- Are the organization's results great—not in financial terms, but in terms of its mission and people?
- Is an organization resilient—can its overall purpose carry it through the really rough times?

- And finally, is an organization's purpose so significant that it could not be replaced if it disappeared?

At Akron Children's, we certainly have a sense of purpose in our mission, and we work daily to be able to answer each of these questions in the affirmative.

Collins knows that the measurement of purpose is rather simple. But do the members of your organization know its purpose? If you ask someone, "Why does this organization exist?" what will he or she tell you? If the answer is "To make money," you know you've got some work to do.

Simply put, a sense of purpose is the hallmark of a strong, healthy organization and another key vital sign.

Organizational Beliefs

The third vital sign of a thriving organization is its *beliefs*.

If purpose tells the members of an organization where it is going, its beliefs are the road map for getting there. By emphasizing certain values and attitudes, an organization tells its members what kinds of actions and approaches are approved for moving toward the group's goals. By making its beliefs clear, an organization indicates the path it expects members to follow.

In his book *A Business and Its Beliefs*, former IBM chief Thomas Watson Jr. relates a core value: "I firmly believe that any organization, in order to survive and achieve success, must have a sound set of behavioral beliefs upon which it premises all its policies and actions."

At Akron Children's, we adopted the Six Pillars of Character as a component of our belief system. These are defined by Character Counts, a nonpartisan, nonsectarian coalition of schools, communities, and organizations working to advance character education.

The Six Pillars of Character are: trustworthiness, respect, responsibility, fairness, caring, and citizenship.

We post these concepts on the walls of our buildings, and we publish them in our internal communications. We discuss them in leadership meetings, and we include them in employee orientation programs and evaluations. We also make an effort to see that our actions support these pillars.

We are also part of "Character Counts! Akron," and we work with the *Akron Beacon Journal* newspaper to recognize young people with character every week. It is second nature for us to think about trustworthiness, respect, responsibility, fairness, caring, and citizenship in all we do.

Is that enough? Frederick Harmon warns that when carefully crafted beliefs are not supported by action, they become empty rhetoric, fostering negativity and cynicism.

Have you noticed that an organization has its own folklore? Every organization, from extended families to Fortune 500 companies, has myths and legends of who did what, and what happened as a result. It is part of any organization's culture. Listen very carefully to those stories. What you are hearing is either the validation or repudiation of that organization's belief system.

Every action an organization takes becomes part of its history. It becomes a piece of evidence, part of an organizational legend that reflects adherence to beliefs.

A couple of clichés can measure this vital sign: Does an organization walk the walk or just talk the talk? And, actions speak louder than words.

The Most Vital Sign

Finally, the fourth vital sign of a thriving organization is *respect*: The simple acknowledgment of each member's worth. I have placed this signpost last because it is the most vital— and the source of a leader's strength.

Have you ever witnessed an organization that seems to hum along efficiently and smoothly? Whether it is a championship team, department, company, or even a church committee, there seems to be some invisible force uniting the team; something that links them as a unit. It's almost as if the silent drumbeat within their veins is synchronized, pounding the same rhythm.

That link is respect.

Respect brings different ideas to the table, which enhances any end product. Respect builds teams, not clones. When you manage by respect—not fear—the results are amazing. It is the great unifier. Respect makes trust possible, reinforces purpose, and gives credibility to beliefs.

If trust is the blood pressure of your organization's heart, respect is its pulse. If it is steady and strong, all the components of an organization can focus on their tasks. If it is weak and erratic, systems begin to fail.

And like pulse, respect is an easy vital sign to observe. You hear it in the voices of your organization's members. You see it in how they treat one another in meetings or at the dinner table. You feel its presence in the harmony of the group. You feel its absence by tension in the air. In fact, this most vital sign is so obvious it is rather difficult to ignore.

Take the four vital signs—trust, purpose, beliefs, respect—to your own organization's heart.

DIGGING DEEPER—SELF-STUDY

- Think of three actions you can take to impart a sense of meaning to your work—and to the work of those around you.

- Do you see evidence that your organization practices internal respect?

- What do your organization's actions say about its values or stated beliefs?

ROLE MODEL

> *"A good leader leads the people from above them.*
> *A great leader leads the people from within them."*
>
> —M. D. Arnold

All leadership books discuss modeling the way. Actions speak louder than words. Talk the talk, walk the walk. You've all heard the discussion and, hopefully, seen its results in action in your organization.

There are leaders who are not good role models, however, and you can learn much from what they could have done differently. Adjust your style accordingly. We've all had good and bad teachers, good and bad coaches.

The trick is to learn valuable lessons from these individuals and not become psychologically damaged by the bad ones. You can protect against damage if you see the problems with this type of leadership and avoid that model in yourself.

Leadership requires excellent role modeling. In a moment, we'll get to some specifics on how to become a role model and more effective leader.

But take a minute now to reflect on your life and the people who shaped who you are. I fondly remember numerous role models who had a profound influence on my life. These were people who cared about me and other people.

My parents are at the top of my list. My dad and mom were married for 68 years. Dad passed away at age 93 and Mom, as I write this, is 90. I'm the oldest of five children, and my childhood memories are nothing short of magical.

For Dad's funeral, we, his children, wrote a poem "He's Our Dad." This verse explained why he was a leader and role model. Mom's verse will be very similar with an additional

Considine Family, 1970. From left, Karen, Howard, Gene, Bill; Mike, Tom, Chris.

focus on her ability to find good in everyone. Mark down that asset—it is truly an essential trait of leadership.

A list of other role models includes my kindergarten teacher, Mrs. Buntz. She was kind and created a welcoming, learning environment, just the thing for a child's first big adventure away from home. She coached, cultivated a desire to learn and care, and had no favorites. She also encouraged nap time, a lesson I still appreciate. Thank you, Mrs. Buntz.

Out of the Comfort Zone

Moving ahead to high school, Brother Leonardo was my sophomore speech instructor. At the time, I prided myself on being a jock—basketball, track, cross-country, soccer, and baseball. He pulled me aside one day and suggested I try out for the school play. The play was *Our Town*. I was cast as Wally Webb. I had a total of 14 words and died in the first act.

The new experience, however, broadened my horizons and provided me with a new appreciation for the arts, and the talent and courage needed by any individual who gets on a stage. That first, small experience gave me the chance to be in musicals, a second school play, and to make numerous new friends.

Brother Leonardo is a role model because he nudged me out of my comfort zone and opened my eyes to new, enriching life experiences.

My list of role models also includes my college soccer coach, Stu Parry, at The University of Akron. Coach Parry definitely walked the walk. He was competitive, fair, encouraging, and honest and had high expectations and standards for himself and everyone around him.

Coach Parry stressed the team, not individuals. He shared the spotlight, was humble and a man of enormous integrity. Sportsmanship in victory or defeat was required. Preparation and personal responsibility for your actions were core ingredients to team chemistry. Communication was clear, concise, and two-way. People were respected and expected to be respectful of others.

The atmosphere allowed for laughter, fun, storytelling, and competition. And it resulted in championships. The foundation he built, starting as a player and coach, culminated in a program that went on to win the NCAA soccer championship in 2010, several years after he retired.

Coach Parry's leadership molded more than all-American soccer players. He molded community leaders who are touching countless lives today through service to others.

During my college years I also served as student government president and witnessed the phenomenal leadership of the university's president, Dr. Norman Auburn. He, again, was a humble man with an eye for attracting and retaining talent. And he was a visionary.

Dr. Auburn could make dreams come true. He had a unique ability to align faculty, administration, students, alumni, the community, state and local governments, donors, and others around a common mission. He was a true role model in every sense of the word, and I still try to practice the lessons I learned from him.

In my junior year in college, a leadership conference for college students in the Omicron Delta Kappa Honor Society was held in Atlanta. Pete Burg, who later became the chief executive officer of FirstEnergy Corp.; Craig Ostergard, who went into real estate in South Carolina; and I were selected to represent the university, joining other students from around the country.

While we were at the conference, Dr. Martin Luther King Jr. was shot and killed in Memphis, Tennessee. The word of that tragedy overwhelmed the conference attendees and redirected our dialogue. We seriously questioned the injustice in our country. We reflected and became even more inspired by Dr. King's words and message. We vowed as a younger generation to get involved in the communities where we lived, to speak out against injustice, and to be solution-focused. We wanted to create communities where different voices could be heard and respected, where children would be safe and could realize their God-given potential and rights.

> *"Life's most persistent and urgent question is, 'What are you doing for others?'"*
>
> —Dr. Martin Luther King Jr.

Dr. King's body was brought to Atlanta, and our conference ended. Yet our personal journey and focus on fulfilling our vow was just beginning.

Connecting Lessons to Life

Many years later, Pete Burg introduced me at a large business gathering and told the story of our Atlanta trip. Pete died of cancer in 2004, however, he stayed true to the vow we made in 1967. My personal leadership efforts have been and continue to be influenced by my vow, Dr. King's words, and that experience.

Graduate school afforded the opportunity for me to delve further into leadership theories and provided opportunities to connect classroom theory with real-life experiences. Fifty years later, 38 of which were spent serving as CEO at Akron Children's Hospital, those experiences increased my interest in the art of leadership.

I've attended numerous conferences, read hundreds of books, learned from observing others, and thought I was thoroughly informed. I was very wrong. I forgot what Mrs. Buntz created as a leader of children by making her classroom a safe zone.

I was reminded of this on April 23, 2014, the day my number one role model, my 93-year-old father, died. The entire family was with him when he took his last breath. My four younger siblings and I, later that day, were talking with one another and the phrase "He's our dad" was continually being used.

From as early as any of us could remember, the words "He's our dad" provided assurance, confidence, parameters, and a safe zone in our lives. We were a family of modest means, yet we never knew what we didn't have, and we knew our small home was a safe place because "He's our dad."

Mom and Dad were active in church, neighborhood, and civic groups, and they took on leadership positions. "Service above self" was their motto, and they set the example for their children. We would often hear strangers told that we were Howard's kids, which established an immediate credibility because of the respect people had for our dad, our role model and leader.

Considine Family, late 1990s. From left, Bill, Chris, Gene, Howard, Mike, Karen, Tom.

Organizational Safe Zones

"He's our dad" was the theme of our eulogy and is still the theme we follow in our daily lives. When we wrote the eulogy, it occurred to me that leaders must create a safe zone for the people in their organizations.

I've had the privilege of being the CEO of a fabulous, mission-driven organization for 38 years. The hospital is 126 years young and now has a workforce of nearly 6,000 people who provided care through more than 1 million patient visits last year. Periodically, when I'm walking through a unit, I'm referred to as "Dad." Since my dad's death, those words have taken on even more meaning.

I also think about leadership and the concept of safe zones. We already have a great culture; when your people are respected, empowered, recognized, and encouraged to innovate, you have a just culture—a safe atmosphere for people to thrive.

Safety does not mean tolerating incompetence, defiance, meanness, and other negative behaviors. Those issues, when addressed, support a safe zone.

As a leader, as the mom or dad of your organization, do you discuss the safe-zone concept? How do you incorporate assurance, trust, and respect in your culture? How do you encourage the people you represent so they have confidence that you will not harm them? Are you transparent in decision making? Are you inclusive and trustworthy? Are you as dedicated to the human spirit as you are to the bottom line?

My dad was that type of leader and father. The words "He's our dad" provide me with inner peace.

I am reminded of an anonymous quote that fits any leadership situation: "Employees do not want a motto, they want a model."

At Akron Children's, we also see role models in our patients and their families, who display courage, persistence, and faith.

I could easily list many more role models, and so can you. Being a role model comes with leadership, so choose to be a positive one. Who are the role models that shaped your life?

Think also about the one trait that all role models and great leaders share. I think it is integrity. Integrity covers values, a sense of self, and honesty. The specifics of leadership all center on being a role model and living your personal values.

Albert Einstein told us, "Try not to become a man of success but rather try to become a man of value."

DIGGING DEEPER—SELF-STUDY

- Make a list of your role models, going back as far as you think appropriate. What did you learn from each?
- What characteristics do you look for in a role model?
- Have you defined your personal "moral compass"—the values you want to represent in your organization?

8

STORYTELLING,

SERVICE

"Storytelling is the most powerful way to put ideas into the world today."

—Robert McKee

STORYTELLING

I have always responded to leaders who are gifted storytellers. They tell stories that serve as examples to the listener. For the best leaders, the stories are not self-promotional or egocentric. The storyteller shows a human side—in fact, this is often the most valuable by-product of a story.

Storytelling influences us every day in the products we buy, the causes we support, and the careers we choose. We all enjoy a good story and understand how it can capture one's undivided attention.

"Stories," said Tahir Shah in *Arabian Nights*, "are a communal currency of humanity."

Every religion has stories of its origin and values. Greek mythology and *Aesop's Fables* provide lessons through stories. Aesop's fable of the tortoise and the hare, for instance, teaches about persistence. Even Jesus made his values known through parables that everyone could understand. Naturally, your organization has stories, true or not, that affect its image.

I've worked in healthcare for 45 years. The true stories that play out daily between patients, families, and caregivers offer tremendous life lessons to everyone. Appropriately sharing those stories can be very powerful.

Telling stories about the proud history and traditions of organizations connects people to the past, honors those who came before, and inspires people to be part of an even brighter future. Leaders can be the bridge between the past, present, and future through storytelling.

Catching the Sun

A powerful story I've shared with many is about the girl you met earlier named Angie. When she was nine years old, in August 1987, Angie was admitted to Akron Children's and diagnosed with acute lymphoid leukemia.

Angie underwent the usual treatment for this particular cancer. The chemotherapy and radiation did their usual damage. What was not usual was Angie's response.

This little girl, whose body endured the worst that cancer and its treatment could throw at her, responded with a positive attitude, smiles, laughter, optimism, and empathy for others. Her spirit became legendary throughout the entire Akron Children's family. Anyone who interacted with Angie came away a better person.

This profoundly ill child reversed our roles. Angie cared for those around her as though we were the sick ones. She took it upon herself to help us heal or, at least, cope. In her spare time, Angie used our art therapy program and supplies her mother brought her to make suncatchers. You've all seen suncatchers hanging in windows, bringing beautiful rays of light into a room. Angie gave those brightly colored panels of plastic and glass to everyone: doctors, visitors, nurses, other patients, and even an administrator or two.

Angie, herself, was a suncatcher. We don't know at what point Angie realized she would never marry, that she would never go to college or even attend a prom. We don't know because she never showed negative thoughts. Suncatchers are like that. They cannot project darkness, only light.

As Jean Luc Godard said, "Sometimes reality is too complex. Stories give it form."

The suncatcher shows another important part of storytelling—recognizing symbols. Akron Children's miracle children are themselves symbols that hold us to high ethical standards and bring honesty to our mission. Your stories also can revolve around a symbol—but a true one, not one made up for convenience.

In his book *Leadership A to Z*, James O'Toole relates a story about Merck, the pharmaceutical company. Merck developed a drug to treat river blindness, which afflicted some 300,000 people in the poorest regions of the world. Against objections from some on its own board, Merck decided to make the drug available for free in those regions—even though it cost $200 million to develop and millions more to distribute.

O'Toole said the monetary cost was more than offset by the morale boost within the corporation. The generosity infused pride within employees, resulting in renewed commitment and loyalty to corporate goals.

Another lesson from O'Toole: Communication takes at least 50 percent of a leader's time. Look for ways to use storytelling to make your organization's values understood by your employees. And remember, like Merck, you can write your own story.

Our Angie would say, a leader must be a suncatcher and bring radiant light into every room and every life that leader enters.

DIGGING DEEPER—SELF-STUDY

- What story would others tell—positive or negative— about your organization?
- Can you think of a symbol—not a logo or a motto—that represents your organization's values?
- Develop three (true) stories that describe your organization.

SERVICE

"To lead people, walk behind them."

—Lao Tzu

Management textbooks and articles have correctly celebrated servant leadership—service above self and similar philosophies—because they work.

A leader who understands the need to serve those he or she leads will be a very effective change agent and steward. A service culture commands respect. Service to others requires sacrifice, patience, and spending time with people. Treat others the way you want to be treated, and people will notice.

Volunteerism in the United States is a significant affirmation of the philosophy of service to others. Through our own experiences, we know the happiness and reward you intrinsically receive when you help someone in need or when you provide service to another person or organization. Random acts of kindness and service are seen routinely in our society, and we truly crave more opportunities.

A service mentality in an organization promotes teamwork and breaks down silos. It promotes honesty, not lies. It promotes putting others before self, and it establishes healthy work environments and thereby, healthy people.

Hospital leaders and clinicians volunteer at a pediatric hospital in Haiti.

Service mentality: What can I do today to help my team? What can I do today to enhance our work environment? What can I do today to enhance customer satisfaction through service to them?

Think service when you think leadership.

The Transformational Leader

Service also implies leading with values and integrity.

Tom Peters and Robert Waterman Jr. were onto something in supporting a values-centered organization. About 50 years ago, leadership became a serious research subject, not only for business and organizational experts but also scholars in sociology, psychology, and communications.

The thrust of these leadership studies has been to move beyond the old, Industrial-Age, top-down leadership style of tightly controlling employees and their tasks. This method is more management than leadership.

And as Peter Drucker tells us, "Management is doing things right; leadership is doing the right things."

The right things in the Knowledge Age include initiating a creative, inclusive, and committed environment for the team and empowering employees to help their leader realize his or her vision for the organization.

James MacGregor Burns, who literally wrote the book *Leadership*, calls this style "transformational leadership." It depends on a leader who has found his or her way and follows a moral compass—those values a leader will not compromise. In this type of organization, leaders act as role models, especially in terms of ethics and values that define the organization.

If all this sounds too New Age to work in a competitive business setting, just look around. Change is coming so fast—to markets, employee adaptability, sustainability, fund-raising— that the world has been described as shifting ground.

In his book *"Entrepreneurial Leadership: A Practical Guide to Generating New Business,"* Angelo Mastrangelo, who teaches leadership and entrepreneurship at Binghamton University in New York, explains that running a successful business requires the leader to "understand and empower others (customers and employees) instead of themselves."

The transformational leader is best suited to build or maintain the kind of service-oriented, innovative, creative, and flexible organization required to weather the 21st century's challenges.

Here are some of the transformational characteristics described by the research:

Leaders serve as role models in terms of ethics and values; they form a vision of where the organization should go and share that with followers; they understand, serve, and empower their teams; and transformational leaders act as change agents for progress. Such leaders initiate a creative, inclusive, and committed environment.

Bill Considine makes friends with a young Haitian child.

One last thing about service, especially where it concerns your values: You can't fake it.

In their leadership study *True North*, Bill George and Peter Sims impart important advice for anyone on a personal leadership journey.

"When you follow your internal compass, your leadership will be authentic," they wrote. "Although others may guide you, your truth is derived from your life story, and only you can determine what it might be."

DIGGING DEEPER—SELF-STUDY

- Recall leaders you have known who embodied servant leadership and those who did not. What did you learn from each?

- How can you practice "random acts of kindness" in your organization?

- When people think of your leadership, do they think service? Ask yourself, why or why not?

9

HUMILITY, HUMOR

"A leader is one who takes a little more than his share of the blame, and a little less than his share of the credit."

—Arnold Glasow

HUMILITY

In the movie *Dave*, Bill Mitchell (played by Kevin Kline) runs a temporary employment agency and happens to look exactly like U.S. President Dave Kovic. Bill ends up serving as president when President Kovic dies. Bill points out in a discussion with his presidential advisors that he is only in a temporary position, which he owes to the people of the country.

Bill shows humility and humanity in every action he takes as chief executive of the country. True leadership embraces humility.

Humility is an important trait of the servant leaders profiled in the previous chapter. These overlapping characteristics also go far in making up the transformational leader I mentioned earlier. Don't underestimate the power of keeping your humanity as you lead your organization.

In their leadership study *Encouraging the Heart*, James Kouzes and Barry Posner discuss the value of caring and encouragement that flow from a leader. One of their five practices for leaders is to simply share accomplishments and credit with those you lead. This practice sets a tone of hope and determination in an organization. From that beginning, loyalty and attention to mission naturally take root.

Caring and humility are necessities in a children's hospital or any healthcare setting. Nurturing is crucial in leading caregivers who deal with patients and families facing serious illness, crises, and grief.

Our patients also keep us humble. We hear their stories, connect with their families and sometimes attend their funerals. And children always see through false humility. Like Angie and her "no time for bad hair days," our miracle children keep us focused on what is important. We humbly go along for the ride and try to keep up with their journeys.

Perhaps your organization's mission is less dramatic. Don't assume that means you have a reduced need to be humble and caring. All workers are stressed, at least part of the time, and sometimes they wonder if their jobs are worth it. A caring attitude helps get people through the rough spots and builds loyalty, morale, and retention.

In addition, having a caring organization doesn't mean you can neglect sound business principles. The Dale Carnegie Institute designed an organizational pyramid that indicates where business solutions come from. At the top of the pyramid are the executives, who produce 6 percent of an organization's solutions to problems. The management group in the middle produces 34 percent. It is the staff members at the bottom of the pyramid who produce 60 percent of an organization's solutions.

Again, people seek value and meaning in their lives. Make them an essential part of your organization. Share, or even direct, the limelight and credit to others. Humble men and women command respect from their team through their interactions—not through titles alone.

Humility fosters credibility, loyalty, and trust. Through humility, a leader becomes a more effective facilitator, coach, and mentor.

We've all witnessed individuals who have let their titles go to their heads. They take credit for all successes and distance themselves from failures. They are viewed as selfish know-it-alls who care about themselves and ignore the needs of others. And they fool no one.

Humility translates to the masses that you are a confident, values-based, caring leader to be trusted and admired. They will give you their support. Humility is essential in leadership.

DIGGING DEEPER—SELF-STUDY

- How does your organization share credit and appreciation with your team?
- Be honest: Are you a humble leader? If so, how do you express it? If not, why not?
- Define actions your organization can take to become a caring organization that practices humility for employees and customers/clients.

HUMOR

"Good humor is a tonic for mind and body. It is the best antidote for anxiety and depression. It is a business asset. It attracts and keeps friends. It lightens human burdens. It is the direct route to serenity and contentment."

—Grenville Kleiser

How does humor fit into the leadership profile? Are we suggesting a leader has to be a comic? Does being humorous suggest you are a silly person who is not serious about the tasks at hand?

These are appropriate questions that highlight the need for balance. I doubt that many true leaders naturally have the humor gene in their DNA. But there are numerous leaders who have mastered the ability to bring humor into their leadership profiles through storytelling and self-effacing examples of their experiences.

Many leaders whom you remember and admire no doubt included humor in their leadership toolboxes. It might be as simple as using humorous quotes to make a point or liven up a speech or a PowerPoint presentation during employee meetings.

An old friend and neighbor of mine was the editor of the local newspaper, the *Akron Beacon Journal*. The late Paul Poorman was naturally funny and used humor to break stress or make his opinion memorable.

Over the years, many reporters and editors entered his corner office to explain a mistake or missed story. Usually, much had gone right, but the story or project failed anyway. For those cases, Paul had a favorite phrase: "Some days you buy a duck, and it drowns."

This was a sign that tensions were diffused, and corrective measures could go forward without blame. When employees feel at ease, they work better. They are empowered to take risks and think creatively. Humor contributes mightily to this atmosphere.

"A sense of humor," said journalist Hugh Sidey, "is needed armor. Joy in one's heart and some laughter on one's lips is a sign that the person, down deep, has a pretty good grasp of life."

Appropriate humor can be an icebreaker, showing the human side of leadership and connecting the leader with a team or audience. Laughing and cracking a smile produce chemical changes in the body that are healthy, create relaxation, and improve awareness, happiness, enhanced listening, and more.

Humor in the Interview

Another friend found an ally in humor when he interviewed for a job as a hospital CEO at a relatively young age. The search committee was comprised of individuals older than he was. It was a very formal setting—somewhat intimidating, structured, and overly polite.

Early in the group questioning, he was asked how he would manage older, talented physicians when he was not a physician himself. He decided to share a story he heard from a mentor—one that captured his philosophy and, at the same time, injected a bit of humor.

He equated the hospital environment to a large circus tent. The featured event at the circus was the lions' show. The lions were talented and good at their work. They came into the cage, mounted their perches, and took turns jumping through rings of fire. The ringmaster orchestrated the performance.

My friend paralleled the ringmaster role with the role of the CEO. People come to the circus to see the lions, just as people come to the hospital to see the doctors. The job of the ringmaster, and that of the CEO, is to make sure the performance is organized and every lion gets to perform. You do not want the confusion of the lions all getting off their pedestals at the same time.

The ringmaster must nurture the lions, provide training and continuous education, feed them well, and direct the applause their way. His whip is for show, and his gun has blanks. The lions are smart and soon figure out that he doesn't use the whip on them and the gun is just noise. Thus, they respond to his style and how they are treated, as individuals and as a team. But if that respect is missing, the lions will get a new ringmaster.

The search committee, physicians, and laypeople had a good laugh over the story and repeated it to others within the organization. A serious question led to a response that mixed humor and revealed a style that embraced teamwork, respect, and collaboration.

Yet another friend interviewed for a hospital CEO position that presented a different situation. He was to follow a person who had been in the job for 35 years. He knew the departing CEO personally, and the search committee asked what advice, if any, he thought the departing executive would give him.

The candidate knew there was some tension around the separation, yet was unsure of the specifics. He obviously did not want to avoid the question or give the impression he would not be his own person. So, he gave the following scenario in response:

> When we got together, Mr. X wished me well. I asked for his sage advice based on his more-than-three decades serving as CEO.
>
> "You'll be fine," he said. "You're well-educated, independent and have a great value system."
>
> "Thanks," I said, "but a few words from you would be most appreciated."
>
> "Okay," he said. "There are three envelopes in the top left-hand desk drawer, numbered one through three. It is important to open them in that order."
>
> He then said that if I found myself in a very tight spot with the board, open the envelope marked

number one. There would be a written suggestion for me to follow.

"Wow." I thanked him, and my job journey began.

The honeymoon period lasted over a year and then, at budget time, a contentious issue dominated the board's discussions. Late at night in the office, preparing for the next day's board meeting, I remembered the envelopes and reached for number one. The message inside read, "Blame it on the previous CEO."

With that suggestion, we packaged a justification for a budget variance on commitments made by the previous CEO, which were out of my control. The storm clouds passed, the budget passed, and smooth sailing returned to my captaincy.

Eighteen months after that, another acrimonious issue affected our strategic planning. My ability to lead was quietly being questioned. In a moment of desperation, I opened envelope number two. It said, "Blame it on the medical staff."

Everyone knows medical staff can be difficult. The phrase "herding cats" comes to mind. If you have 400 doctors, you have 400 opinions. So the answer to that problem was "the medical staff." Everyone accepted them as the barrier. I was out of the woods and still sailing the ship.

Soon after that, another issue raised its ugly head and I was expected to come up with a resolution—one that would be a win-win for all parties. Again, I was in a corner, and again I opened the envelope—number three. The message simply said, "Prepare three letters."

The search committee loved the story, enjoyed the humor, and concluded their candidate was not going to play the blame game or make excuses for his actions. In those cases, appropriate humor helped define a leadership profile that people would respond to and respect.

Finding Humor

One might well agree that humor is important in most organizations but wonder, "How do you find humor in a children's hospital?" In one sense, a hospital is the last place you might expect to find humor—but it is the first place where humor is essential.

A sense of humor is crucial for getting through stressful situations, which are found in hospitals and all other organizations. That doesn't mean you have to walk around telling the joke of the day or, worse, playing practical jokes. Your role is to find ways to lighten the mood and provide an atmosphere in which people—employees, customers, clients—feel at ease. And you never know where you might find the answer.

For instance, a recently retired Akron Children's staff member left a lasting legacy, even though she didn't perform extraordinary surgery or find a cure for disease. Marilyn McGuckin joined Akron Children's in 1983 as the director of volunteer services. She developed many

Marilyn McGuckin founded Akron Children's beloved Doggie Brigade.

important programs to promote interactions between staff, families, and, of course, our kids.

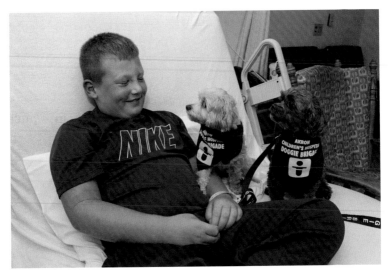

Doggie Brigade members hard at work.

There is one program, however, that everyone connects with—Akron Children's Doggie Brigade, which Marilyn founded in 1992. Specially trained dogs and their owners are frequent visitors to our hospital's halls and special events. The dogs don't have to do tricks, they are just a calming, welcome presence for the ill children and their families.

The dogs make everyone smile and, being dogs, they seem to know which children need their attention the most. The Doggie Brigade raises the mood of everyone in the hospital and provides a fun, caring sense of connection. This provides common ground and a shared interest that makes the journey a bit brighter.

In using humor to be a better leader, you don't have to be a comic. But you might be wise to look for your own Doggie Brigade-type idea.

DIGGING DEEPER—SELF-STUDY

- Can you recall examples of using humor to make a point or defuse a situation?
- What have you learned from occasions in which inappropriate humor—yours or other leaders—misfired?
- When you see leaders use humor wisely, do you find ways to incorporate those techniques into your own style?

10

IMPROVEMENT,
INTELLECTUAL
INDEPENDENCE

"Strive for continuous improvement, instead of perfection."

—Kim Collins

IMPROVEMENT

When I was contemplating writing this book, I shared the concept with a colleague, Dr. Uma Kotagal, senior vice president for quality and transformation and director of the Center for Health Policy and Clinical Effectiveness at Cincinnati Children's Hospital Medical Center. Dr. Kotagal is a phenomenal woman with a passion for assuring a safe and quality experience for every child being admitted to a hospital. Her belief system: Do no harm. Heal the illness. Ensure the child is safe and respected.

She is known internationally for her advocacy, and she is one of my heroes.

When I told her how I think about leadership and apply words to every letter in order to monitor my style, she said without hesitation, "I hope *improvement* is one of your *I* words."

I thank Uma for her reminder and suggestion because leadership is all about improvement. Status quo is our worst enemy. Improvement must be the first priority of a leader—improvement of process, people, and self.

A Culture of Improvement

The concept of a leader setting the stage and leading a culture of improvement was ingrained in my philosophy through the experience of a nine-year-old at Akron Children's. I was CEO during her experience and during many discussions with her family after the young girl's death.

The child is the same Angie you met earlier and whose spirit lives in the pages of this book, as well as in our organization's values. You might remember Angie was diagnosed with acute lymphoid leukemia, went through treatment, and met the worst that cancer and invasive treatment could throw at her with smiles, optimism, and empathy toward others.

Her spirit became legendary throughout the entire hospital family. We tried to make her better, but Angie was the one who made everyone else better, through her interaction with others and the force of her personality.

You may recall that part of that interaction came in the form of suncatchers she made in our art therapy program—brightly colored panels of plastic and glass that she gave to doctors, nurses, visitors, other patients, and administrators. Many suncatchers still hang in windows around the hospital, brightening rooms and work areas.

But Angie lives on in other tangible ways. Incredibly, she wasn't finished teaching us when she died at the age of 13.

Following her death, her mom Joyce wrote me a letter. The hospital had become a home away from home for Joyce, her husband David, and their family. In fact, the caregivers had become a real part of Angie's family.

A Spirit of Improvement

Joyce was thankful in her letter for our care, but suggested that we could be better. We could improve. We needed to be continuous learners. She proposed a parents' advisory board at the hospital. It was a great idea, and we lost no time adopting it.

From that initiative and from Joyce's leadership a parents' mentoring program developed and has helped innumerable families deal with the effects of illness and death. Today, we have more than 100 mentors reaching out to families on a daily basis, and we have a very active parent advisory group.

At the one-year celebration of our Parent Advisory Council, Joyce presented me with a special gift—one of Angie's suncatchers. This particular work was special because it was one of two that were not finished before Angie's death. The corner panels had not been painted with their vibrant colors.

Joyce kept one of those suncatchers at home to remind her that her work as Angie's mom would never be done. She does a great job of keeping that spirit alive.

She thought the second unfinished suncatcher belonged at Akron Children's. It hangs in my office to remind me every day that our work will never be done. We need to keep Angie's spirit alive through our activities.

As Joyce told me at the presentation, "Angie always had a smile, no matter how tough life became, and I believe her smile is reflected in this suncatcher she created. When you look at it, remember her life, and then think about how this one life has made a difference for so many people."

Angie's suncatcher hangs in Bill Considine's office as a reminder of her spirit and the unfinished work left to be done.

Leadership Crucibles

In any leader's development there are down periods in which you might not feel you or your organization is improving. Leadership expert Bill George calls these times "crucibles." He means a difficult period at work or home that tests you, often to the core.

The good news is that crucibles can transform your view of what leadership and life are all about. George found that crucibles are normally followed by a "rapid acceleration" in your leadership development. This is all part of being a values-oriented leader whose personal improvement benefits the organization.

Angie did not teach me how to run a hospital, but she taught me how to live a better life. She taught me courage and perseverance. She taught me charity, compassion, and perspective. And she taught me there is no time for bad hair days in our profession.

Almost 20 years have passed, yet the light from the suncatcher her mother gave me has not dimmed. It has been magnified.

Angie and the dozens of other suncatchers who have graced my life restore something good in me. They are a remedy for cynicism and windows of light in the hours of gloom. They bring me through the crucibles I encounter. They are my heroes.

Finally, Angie and her family taught me the importance of improving daily. That mind-set and my work with Dr. Kotagal have led to a national quality and safety initiative at a network of children's hospitals around the nation, seeking to eliminate errors and unintentional harm to patients.

We are striving for "zero" errors.

DIGGING DEEPER—SELF-STUDY

- What is your organization's conscious, planned strategy for continuous improvement?
- Are your employees and clients/customers a part of your improvement plans?
- Think of ways you can ingrain a culture of improvement in your organization.

INTELLECTUAL INDEPENDENCE

> *"If you look to lead, invest at least 40 percent of your time in leading yourself—your own purpose, ethics, principles, motivation, conduct."*
>
> —Dee Hock

Our current political system is paralyzed by partisanship. Regardless of the side legislators are on, they are pressured to stay together as a party against the other side.

Simply put, this is not leadership. Politicians owe us their independent judgment, based on a nonbiased study of the facts, personal integrity, and service to all.

Leadership requires an intellectual independence not controlled by the latest fad, peer pressure, or ill-intentioned individuals. Intellectual independence creates trust in those who look to a leader for direction. A leader with mental independence is open to ideas from all sources and finds solutions to implement that are in the best interest of the public good.

Intellectual independence requires courage, compromise, collaboration, and communication. Leaders who have excellent intellectual ability and an independent open-thought process are approachable and solution-oriented. They are not puppets of someone else's agenda.

Leaders who become puppets lose their ability to lead. People soon figure out that these individuals either can't or won't be open-minded, and they quit bringing them ideas. People—the leader's team—find ways to work around puppets. As they correctly reason, why not just attempt to find the person pulling the strings and try to influence him or her?

Rise Above Puppetry

To avoid being a puppet, a leader must reject strict ideology and learn to question outmoded procedures. Independent leaders are thinking leaders. We have many scientists in our hospital—doctors, medical researchers, and lab technicians. Maybe you have a research and development group, also.

We have much to learn from these scientists. Consider again the basics of the scientific method: study a problem, theorize a solution, test, and retest. Be prepared to adjust your position or your course of action in light of new facts or information gained.

Remember, however, to adjust your strategy only. Don't adjust or compromise your values.

We've all worked with people who are referred to as their own person because they live by their values. They don't flip-flop their beliefs. Intellectual independence must have a positive focus and be generous where others are concerned.

As I've mentioned, finding your core values and beliefs is a personal journey. Bill George, in his book *True North*, writes that a leader's development is not a straight line or a race, but a marathon with detours and varied terrain. To be true to yourself, you must first define yourself.

George describes a leader's early years—up to age 30—as a time to be "rubbing up against the world" or getting to know yourself. The chronological age might vary, but the point is that early in your leadership career you must come to know your value system. Otherwise, you'll spend your career serving the interests of others—in short, being a puppet.

Before you can become a true, independent leader, you must set your values.

"Do what you feel in your heart to be right," Eleanor Roosevelt once said, "for you'll be criticized anyway."

Leaders with intellectual independence can ask the tough question or make the unpopular yet correct decision. Because of the trust and credibility these leaders have built, their followers believe in them and respect their positions.

DIGGING DEEPER—SELF-STUDY

- Write down three to five personal values that, as a leader, you will not compromise.
- Do your values fit with your organization's mission and practices?
- How can you better "lead yourself" toward making values-based leadership decisions?

11

PRIVILEGE, PEOPLE

"Leadership is an opportunity that many identify as a burden, when in fact, it should be truly seen as a privilege."

—Billy D. Hayes

PRIVILEGE

James is a piano prodigy who has performed in international competitions since he was six years old. A few years ago, after a whirlwind performance schedule that included stops in Paris and New York's Carnegie Hall, James put his music travels on hold. He had been diagnosed with Ewing's sarcoma, a rare bone cancer.

As his family was moving to Ohio, James complained of nagging abdominal pain so his

James Wilson, 2016

family brought him to Akron Children's Hospital for doctors to treat the golf-ball-size tumor in his stomach.

During his stay at Akron Children's, our music therapist Sarah Gaither made sure a keyboard was always available for James to play. He returned the favor by practicing with an open door so others could hear and be soothed by the sounds of Mozart and Beethoven.

After chemotherapy shrank the tumor, pediatric surgeon Aaron Garrison and his team removed it. James's outlook is good. On the day of his surgery, Dr. Garrison and the entire operating room team prepped while watching a YouTube video of James performing.

James performs classical music for patients and staff during one of his hospital stays.

"I wanted everyone to step back and realize how important our job is," Dr. Garrison said, "and how lucky we are to help kids like James."

Leadership is a privileged role.

Individuals who simply do not understand the meaning of that privilege ultimately violate an essential trust, rendering their leadership useless.

Granted, the privilege often is not as dramatic as saving the lives and futures of children. But the privilege of leadership has numerous rewards and, at the same time, numerous responsibilities.

"The price of greatness," Winston Churchill said, "is responsibility."

Earning the Privilege

Privilege cannot be taken for granted. As already mentioned earlier, this privilege needs to be earned at every turn. The constant mental reminder that leading is a privilege will help you model your behavior. It should be part of your toolbox: Put a personal value on this privileged role and strive to grow it within your value account.

Author and playwright George Bernard Shaw spoke to his own idea of privilege:

> "I am of the opinion that my life belongs to the whole community and, as long as I live, it is my privilege to do for it whatever I can.
>
> "I rejoice in life for its own sake. Life is no brief candle for me.
>
> "It is a sort of splendid torch, which I have got hold of for a moment, and I want to make it burn as brightly as possible before handing it on to future generations."

Bill George, who interviewed numerous leaders to track authentic leadership traits, found leadership to be a journey, not a destination. And the privilege of leadership involves giving back to those you lead.

Life coaches sometimes conduct an exercise in which clients write their own obituaries. The lesson: When you look back on your life's accomplishments, what will they be? Will you only have a list of titles you have held or will you have a solid indication that you stuck to your values and appreciated those around you?

Remember, there is a difference between being a privileged person and being someone who knows leadership itself is a privilege.

As leaders of value and humility, we must, as John F. Kennedy said, "Make sure the light from the torch that is passed to you burns even brighter when you pass it on."

DIGGING DEEPER—SELF-STUDY

- Do you understand the privilege of leadership? How do you express it in your actions?
- What legacy will you leave to future leaders in your organization?

PEOPLE

"I've learned that people will forget what you said, people will forget what you did, but people will never forget how you made them feel."

—Maya Angelou

People are at the core of leadership interaction.

You do not need a textbook, degree, or seminar to appreciate the fact that leadership is about people. People power has proven itself time and time again.

In the 1960s, a youth volunteer singing group toured college campuses under the name "Up with People." Their signature song, also called "Up with People," included a chorus about the value of genuinely caring about other people.

This song from the past illustrated for me the necessity of having leaders who care about people. This has been a theme throughout this book, and it must be a core value and belief of any successful leader.

Leaders who concentrate on their personal success, their bonus, the bottom line, often lose the essential connection with people. Business performance is obviously important. Yet when it comes at the expense of people and their well-being, leadership fails.

People Power

Don't forget, people power is the basis of democracy. It takes us back to the Jeffersonian ideal that if you give people information and responsibility, they will generally make the right decisions.

People also are at the heart of any discussion on values, including perhaps the oldest value: the Golden Rule. Simply treat others the way you wish to be treated. Serve and even love those you lead.

No doubt a lot of organizations pay lip service to the mantra that people are the most important product. But people power is a reality leaders should embrace.

As Steve Jobs, the late CEO of Apple, often said, "It does not make sense to hire smart people and then tell them what to do. We hire smart people so that they can tell us what to do."

Empowering people is the most efficient way to meet many organizations' biggest challenge: change. Thomas Friedman writes of the future world as "hot, flat and crowded," with a constantly changing social and economic landscape. The ground is shifting beneath organizations. In such cases an adaptable team is the best, most consistent asset.

One way to serve your people—and your organization—is by training and retraining your people to meet any challenge. Peter Drucker sees this lifelong learning as simply the "process of keeping abreast of change."

Much recent leadership research promotes the concept of employees as a team, inspired by a values-centered leader who practices respect and trust. That's just good business.

One example experts point to is the visionary company, Starbucks. The Starbucks mission statement includes six principles. The very first principle:

"Provide a great work environment and treat each other with respect."

Starbucks and other successful companies thrive because their associates are invested in the work and the mission.

So, people power is a two-way street between leaders and their people. A leader who has a love for his or her people will thrive.

Simon Sinek has said, "When we work hard on something we believe in, it's called passion. When we work hard on something we don't believe in, it's called stress."

Love your people as a leader.

DIGGING DEEPER—SELF-STUDY

- What people power goals are built into your organization?
- Do you empower those you lead to be a part of major decisions?
- Is your team trained and prepared to be adaptable to changing conditions within your industry?

ACKNOWLEDGMENT

I am extremely grateful to everyone who made the publication of this book possible. I wish to thank Ron Kirksey for his help producing the manuscript. His guidance in taking the concept for the book from thought to text was invaluable. I also owe a debt of gratitude to Ted Stevens for providing many of the photographs. Ted has captured many magic moments over the years as a photographer at Akron Children's Hospital.

I am especially indebted to all the teachers and mentors who helped shape my views on leadership and shared their insights with me throughout my career. I consider myself fortunate to have been associated with Akron Children's Hospital for 38 years. It has been a privilege to work alongside our wonderful staff, donors, board members and community partners, and I will always treasure the lessons I have learned from the patients and families we serve.

ABOUT THE AUTHOR

William H. Considine, CEO of Akron Children's Hospital for 38 years, has dedicated both his career and personal life to improving pediatric care and the quality of life for children and families. He is one of the longest-tenured hospital chief executives in the country and is an internationally known advocate for issues affecting children's health and well-being. He is widely consulted by policy makers in Columbus and Washington, D.C., and he has served on the boards of many healthcare, educational, and cultural organizations.

Under his leadership, the hospital has grown into one of the nation's premier independent, integrated pediatric healthcare delivery systems. Akron Children's today is a $1 billion enterprise with nearly 6,000 employees. Its clinical staff provides care through more than one million patient visits annually via its programs at two hospital campuses and a network of more than 60 primary, urgent care, and specialty care locations. The system also comprises a pediatric home care company, school health program, captive insurance entity, and charitable foundation.

Considine is a Fellow in the American College of Healthcare Executives. He is a past chairman of the National Association of Children's Hospitals and Related Institutions, and served as a member of its Council on Child Advocacy. He served as chairman of the Child Health Corporation of America and was a member of the American Hospital Association's Maternal Child Health Governing Council. He is a member of the Children's Hospital Association, and he currently serves as chairman of the Ohio Children's Hospital Association. He is a past chairman of the Children's Miracle Network board and served on the Governor's Advisory Council on Health Care Payment Innovation, as well as the Ohio Hospital Association's Task Force on Healthcare Transformation.

In 2009, Considine was inducted into the Northeast Ohio Business Hall of Fame. He is a member of the Ohio Business Roundtable and was appointed to the board of the John S. and James L. Knight Foundation in 2011. Considine continues to serve on the boards of numerous Akron-area community organizations and has been honored by many of these, including the American Lung Association, March of Dimes, Mental Health Association of Summit County, Akron Public Schools, and many others. In 2011, the Akron Community Foundation presented him with the Bert A. Polsky Humanitarian Award in recognition of his many years of community service. In 2014, both the United Way and Akron Children's Hospital presented Considine with their Distinguished Service Awards.

Considine has been honored by his high school alma mater, Archbishop Hoban High School, as well as The University of Akron, where he received his undergraduate degree in 1969. He served as a lieutenant in the United States Public Health Service and holds a master's degree in health science administration from The Ohio State University. He has received two honorary degrees: a doctorate in humane letters from The University of Akron and a doctor of science (honoris causa) from Northeast Ohio Medical University.

Throughout his entire career in healthcare, he has embraced the philosophy of servant leadership. He has consistently been a proactive voice for children, a trusted mentor, an exemplary role model, and an engaging storyteller. Akron Children's

Hospital has a proud 126-year history of caring for children, and the hospital's mission of service has thrived under his guidance.

Considine lives in Akron with Rebecca, his wife of 44 years. They have three grown children and two grandchildren.

From left, Michael, Bill, Becky, Cathryn (Considine) O'Malley, Jemma O'Malley, Michael O'Malley, Graeme O'Malley, Matthew Considine.

ABOUT AKRON CHILDREN'S HOSPITAL

Akron Children's Hospital is ranked among the best children's hospitals by *U.S. News & World Report*. With more than one million patient visits in 2016, Akron Children's has been leading the way to healthier futures for children through quality patient care, education, advocacy, community service, and medical discovery since 1890. The system is the largest pediatric provider in northeast Ohio and is comprised of two hospital campuses and more than 60 urgent, primary, and specialty care locations. The system is proud of its partnerships with other health systems to bring its neonatal and pediatric expertise to patients in their community hospitals, while its home care and school health nurses care for kids in their homes and schools. Learn more at akronchildrens.org.

BIBLIOGRAPHY

Autry, James. A. *Love and Profit: The Art of Caring Leadership*. New York: Morrow, 1991.

Burns, James MacGregor. *Leadership*. New York: Harper & Row, 1978.

Collins, James C. *Good to Great: Why Some Companies Make the Leap ... and Others Don't*. New York: Harper Business, 2001.

Collins, James C., and Porras, Jerry I. *Built to Last: Successful Habits of Visionary Companies*. New York: Harper Business, 1994.

Friedman, Thomas L. *Hot, Flat, and Crowded*. New York: Picador, 2009.

Fulghum, Robert. *All I Really Need to Know I Learned in Kindergarten: Uncommon Thoughts on Common Things*. New York: Villard, 1988.

George, Bill, and Peter Sims. *True North: Discover Your Authentic Leadership*. San Francisco: Jossey-Bass/John Wiley & Sons, 2007.

Harmon, Frederick G. *Playing for Keeps: How the World's Most Aggressive and Admired Companies Use Core Values to Manage, Energize, and Organize Their People and Promote, Advance, and Achieve Their Corporate Missions*. New York: John Wiley & Sons, 1996.

Kouzes, James M., and Posner, Barry Z. *Encouraging the Heart: A Leader's Guide to Rewarding and Recognizing Others*. San Francisco: Jossey-Bass, 1999. Print.

Lewin, Roger, and Regine, Birute. *The Soul at Work: Listen, Respond, Let Go: Embracing Complexity Science for Business Success*. New York: Simon & Schuster, 2000.

Mastrangelo, Angelo. *Entrepreneurial Leadership: A Practical Guide to Generating New Business*. Santa Barbara, CA: ABC-CLIO, LLC, 2016.

O'Toole, James. *Leadership A to Z: A Guide for the Appropriately Ambitious*. San Francisco: Jossey-Bass, 1999.

Peters, Tom, and Waterman, Robert H. *In Search of Excellence: Lessons from America's Best-run Companies*. Cambridge, MA, and London: Harper & Row, 1982.

Termini, Michael J. *Walking the Talk: Moving into Leadership*. Dearborn, MI: Society of Manufacturing Engineers, 2007.

Watson, Thomas J. *A Business and Its Beliefs; the Ideas That Helped Build IBM*. New York: McGraw-Hill, 1963.

INDEX

Italic page numbers indicate photos